Wilt Thou Go With This Man?

Wilt Thou Go With This Man?

Gospel Sermons preached during the 1859 Awakening

BROWNLOW NORTH

The Banner of Truth Trust
78b Chiltern Street, London, W1

First published under the title Yes! or No! *1867*

First Banner of Truth Trust edition 1966

Set in 11/12 Times Roman and
Printed and Bound in Great Britain by
Hazell Watson & Viney Ltd
Aylesbury, Bucks

Contents

NOTE

It will be noted that in his Scripture quotations the author sometimes departs from the exact wording of the Authorized Version. This is because he was quoting from memory.

AND ABRAHAM WAS OLD, AND WELL STRICKEN IN age: and the Lord had blessed Abraham in all things. And Abraham said unto his eldest servant of his house, that ruled over all that he had, Put, I pray thee, thy hand under my thigh: and I will make thee swear by the Lord, the God of heaven, and the God of the earth, that thou shalt not take a wife unto my son of the daughters of the Canaanites, among whom I dwell: but thou shalt go unto my country, and to my kindred, and take a wife unto my son Isaac.

'And the servant said unto him, Peradventure the woman will not be willing to follow me unto this land: must I needs bring thy son again unto the land from whence thou camest?

'And Abraham said unto him, Beware thou that thou bring not my son thither again. The Lord God of heaven, which took me from my father's house, and from the land of my kindred, and which spake unto me, and that sware unto me, saying, Unto thy seed will I give this land; he shall send his angel before thee, and thou shalt take a wife unto my son from thence. And if the woman will not be willing to follow thee, then thou shalt be clear from this my oath: only bring not my son thither again. And the servant put his hand under the thigh of Abraham his master, and sware to him concerning that matter.

'And the servant took ten camels of the camels of his master, and departed; for all the goods of his master *were* in his hand: and he arose and went to Mesopotamia, unto the city of Nahor. And he made his camels to kneel down without the city by a well of water at the time of the evening, *even* the time that women go out to draw *water*.

'And he said, O Lord God of my master Abraham, I pray thee, send me good speed this day, and show kindness unto my master Abraham. Behold, I stand *here* by the well of water; and the daughters of the men of the city come out to draw water: and let it come to pass, that the damsel to whom I shall say, Let down thy pitcher, I pray thee, that I may drink; and she shall say, Drink, and I will give thy camels drink also: *let the same be* she *that* thou hast appointed for thy servant Isaac; and thereby shall I know that thou hast showed kindness unto my master.

'And it came to pass, before he had done speaking, that, behold, Rebekah came out (who was born to Bethuel, son of Milcah, the wife of Nahor, Abraham's brother), with her pitcher upon her shoulder. And the damsel *was* very fair to look upon, a virgin, neither had any man known her: and she went down to the well, and filled her pitcher, and came up. And the servant ran to meet her, and said, Let me, I pray thee, drink a little water of thy pitcher. And she said, Drink, my lord: and she hasted, and let down her pitcher upon her hand, and gave him drink. And when she had done giving him drink, she said, I will draw *water* for thy camels also, until they have done drinking. And she hasted, and emptied her pitcher into the trough, and ran again unto the well to draw *water*, and drew for all his camels. And the man wondering at her held his peace, to wit, whether the LORD had made his journey prosperous or not.

'And it came to pass, as the camels had done drinking, that the man took a golden earring [*or,* jewel for the forehead] of half a shekel weight, and two bracelets for her hands of ten *shekels* weight of gold; and said, Whose daughter *art* thou? tell me, I pray thee: is there room *in* thy father's house for us to lodge in? And she said unto him, I *am* the daughter of Bethuel the son of Milcah, which she bare unto Nahor. She said moreover unto him, We have both straw and provender enough, and room to lodge in. And the man bowed down his head, and worshipped the LORD. And he said, Blessed *be* the LORD God of my master Abraham, who hath not left destitute my master of his mercy and his truth: I *being* in the way, the Lord led me to the house of my master's brethren.

'And the damsel ran, and told *them* of her mother's house these things. And Rebekah had a brother, and his name *was* Laban: and Laban ran out unto the man, unto the well. And it came to pass, when he saw the earring, and bracelets upon his sister's hands, and when he heard the words of Rebekah his sister, saying, Thus spake the man unto me; that he came unto the man; and, behold, he stood by the camels at the well. And he said, Come in, thou blessed of the LORD; wherefore standest thou without? for I have prepared the house, and room for the camels. And the man came into the house: and he ungirded his camels, and gave straw and provender for the camels, and water to wash his feet, and the men's feet that *were* with him. And there was set *meat* before him to eat: but he said, I will not eat, until I have told mine errand. And he said, Speak on.

'And he said, I *am* Abraham's servant. And the Lord hath blessed my master greatly; and he is become great: and He hath given him flocks, and herds, and silver, and gold, and menservants, and maidservants, and camels, and asses. And Sarah my master's wife bare a son to my master when she was old: and unto him hath he given all that he hath. And my master made me swear, saying, Thou shalt not take a wife to my son of the daughters of the Canaanites, in whose land I dwell: but thou shalt go unto my father's house, and to my kindred, and take a wife unto my son. And I said unto my master, Peradventure the woman will not follow me. And he said unto me, The LORD, before whom I walk, will send his angel with thee, and prosper thy way; and thou shalt take a wife for my son of my kindred, and of my father's house: then shalt thou be clear from *this* my oath, when thou comest to my kindred; and if they give not thee *one,* thou shalt be clear from my oath. And I came this day unto the well, and said, O LORD God of my master Abraham, if now thou do prosper my way which I go: behold, I stand by the well of water; and it shall come to pass, that when the virgin cometh forth to draw *water,* and I say to her, Give me, I pray thee, a little water of thy pitcher to drink; and she say to me, Both drink thou, and I will also draw for thy camels: *let* the same *be* the woman whom the LORD hath appointed out for my master's son. And before I had done speaking in mine heart, behold, Rebekah came forth with her pitcher on her shoulder; and she went down unto the well, and drew *water:* and I said unto her, Let me drink, I pray thee. And she made haste, and let down her pitcher from her *shoulder,* and said, Drink, and I will give thy camels drink also: so I drank, and she made the camels drink also. And I asked her, and said, Whose daughter art thou? And she said, The daughter of Bethuel, Nahor's son, whom Milcah bare unto him: and I put the earring upon her face, and the bracelets upon her hands. And I bowed down my head and worshipped the LORD, and blessed the LORD God of my master Abraham, which had led me in the right way to take my master's brother's daughter unto his son. And now if ye will deal kindly and truly with my master, tell me: and if not, tell me; that I may turn to the right hand, or to the left.

'Then Laban and Bethuel answered and said, The thing proceedeth from the Lord: we cannot speak unto thee bad or good. Behold, Rebekah *is* before thee, take *her,* and go, and let her be thy master's son's wife, as the LORD hath spoken. And it came to pass, that, when Abraham's servant heard their words, he worshipped the LORD, *bowing himself* to the earth. And the servant brought forth jewels of silver, and jewels of gold, and raiment, and *gave* them to Rebekah: he gave also to her brother and to her mother precious things. And they did eat and drink, he and the men that *were* with him, and tarried all night; and they rose up in the morning, and he said, Send me away unto my master. And her brother and her mother said, Let the damsel abide with us *a few* days, at the least ten; after that she shall go. And he said unto them, Hinder me not, seeing the LORD hath prospered my way; send me away that I may go to my master. And they said, We will call the damsel, and enquire at her mouth. And they called Rebekah, and said unto her, Wilt thou go with this man? And she said, I will go.'

1: The Offer

'And they called Rebekah, and said unto her, Wilt thou go with this man? And she said, I will go.' Genesis 24:58.

THE CHAPTER FROM WHICH THIS VERSE IS TAKEN explains the object for which Abraham sent his servant into Mesopotamia: to seek a bride for his master's son. Now my object in sending this little book into the world is to seek a bride for my Master's Son. I profess to be a servant of the God and Father of our Lord and Saviour Jesus Christ; and as Abraham's servant went to Rebekah, and in the name and by the command of Abraham, asked her to enter into a marriage covenant with Isaac, so I come to you, in the name and by the command of Abraham's God, and offer you union with the Lord Jesus Christ.

'Wilt thou go with this man' – the Man Christ Jesus? The question thus put may be abrupt and startling, but, nevertheless, a more real or genuine offer was never made. God helping me, I will tell you more about Jesus and His offer presently, but I begin with this statement: no matter what you have been or what you are, if you will accept Jesus, Jesus will accept you. Only let God hear you say what Abraham's servant heard Rebekah say and this very instant, for better for worse, for richer for poorer, in sickness and in health, His people to be your people, and His God your God, Christ is yours, and you are His. 'They called Rebekah, and said unto her, Wilt thou go with this man? And she said, I will go.' By the power of the Holy Ghost, may you answer as she did.

In commencing to speak or write on spiritual subjects, an oppressive feeling is often on me, not only personally painful, but paralysing – so paralysing that it seems to hinder the full expression of much that I would say. I know that if God teaches me (and I have His promise that, if I ask Him, He will), truth will go forth from me, whenever I speak or write in His name, of more value than a thousand worlds – truth that is bread for the living, and life for the dead. But I also know that, as it was in the days of Moses, so it is too likely to be now – the Word preached will not profit multitudes, not being mixed with faith in them that hear it (Heb. 4:2).

If you, reader, are an unsaved man, or an unsaved woman, there is that in this little book of mine of more value to you than health, or wealth, or honours, or father, or mother, or children, or wife, or even your own life; it contains an offer to you which, if accepted, will bring you into union with One who is able to supply every need you have, not for this world only, but for eternity. In His treasury are good things which it has not entered into the heart of man to conceive – and amongst these good things, He is himself the pearl of great price, the richest treasure amongst them all; and not only these treasures, *but Himself also* He offers you, if you will take Him. Oh, wilt thou not go with this Man?

At present you are without Christ, and if without Christ, then Satan, the god of this world, is leading you with blinded eyes down the broad road that leads to destruction; you have 'no hope,' and are 'without God in the world.' (2 Cor. 4:4; Eph. 2:12). You may have temporal comforts, and temporal hopes; you may even have some false spiritual hopes, but for all that, there is no creature out of hell more poor, more needy, more miserable than you are. You may have much temporal goods laid up for many years, but any day your soul may be required of you; and what will it profit you, though you have gained the whole world, if you have lost your own soul? When this world is over it will matter little what portion you had of its good things; but when it is passed, it will matter a great deal where you spend the eternity on which you must then enter. Believe it, or not, there is an eternity before you; and unless you acquaint yourself now with God, unless you believe in His offers of pardon, and mercy, and love; unless you believe in the offer He makes you of His son, and, believing it, accept it, you must spend that eternity with the devil and his angels.

This may seem to you dreamy and unreal; and the fear that it will surely appear so to many who read these pages is the cause of the painful and paralysing feelings of which I spoke. It is awful to see men rushing headlong to destruction, rejecting the counsel of God against themselves; but, reject it or not, what I tell you is the truth of God, and I do ask and beseech you, as you would not at the last be found a sinner against your own soul, to give this book diligent, careful, and above all prayerful consideration. The Bereans searched the Scriptures daily to see whether the things spoken by Paul were so; therefore, says the Holy Spirit, many of them believed. (Acts 17:11, 12). May the same Spirit put it into your heart to act like the Bereans.

Before Rebekah could by any possibility have been prevailed upon to leave her father's house, and start with Abraham's servant on that unknown wilderness journey, there was one thing of which she must have been perfectly satisfied. What was it? Think for a moment – what was absolutely necessary for Rebekah to believe, before she would for one instant entertain the proposition made her? Rebekah required to be fully persuaded in her own mind *that there was such a person as Isaac.*

Rebekah was suddenly invited to forsake all she had – old ways, old faces, old places, old customs, old connec-

14

tions; father, mother, brother, home, relations, friends, all were to be abandoned; and she was asked to start on a long and wearisome journey, to be the bride of one she had never seen, on the assurance of his servant that he was blessed of God, and would be a blessing to her. Now I say she would require at least to be persuaded that Isaac was a person who really existed, before she would even listen to any such proposal. But Rebekah had no doubt of it; though she had never seen him, she had no more doubt of the existence of Isaac than she had of her own existence; nay, more, it is evident from her whole conduct that she not only believed him to be a real person, but also believed all the good of him which his faithful servant had told her. And this faith it was which enabled her to break at once from old habits and old ties; to leave her father's house, and face the wilderness journey. 'And they called Rebekah, and said unto her, Wilt thou go with this man? And she said, I will go.'

As it was with Rebekah, so it is with you. As Abraham's servant asked her, so I ask you to give yourself to One whom you have never seen. I will presently try and tell you of the love of Him with whom I ask you to go: and, pointing out the blessedness of the offer, and the madness past expression of rejecting it, urge you with all my might to do as did Rebekah; but unless you listen to what I say with as much faith as enables you to believe that the offer is real – that there literally is such a person as Jesus Christ and that if you now accept Him and start on your journey to go to Him, the hour will surely arrive when your own eyes will see Him, and your own ears hear His voice of welcome – my labour will be in vain. 'Without faith,' says the Scripture, 'it is impossible to please him: for he that cometh to God must believe that he is, and that he is a rewarder of them that diligently seek him.' (Heb. 11 : 6). Now, though the Scripture declares that thus much faith

15

at least is absolutely necessary to salvation, for without it, it is 'impossible to please Him,' how many are there who would think it most uncharitable to say they were not Christians, yet who have never examined themselves whether they have this faith – who have never examined whether they have as much faith as enables them to believe that there really is such a Person as Jesus Christ!

Examine yourself! Perhaps you will find more in what I have just said than at first sight may appear to you. A man will be a Christian just so far as he thinks it worth his while; or, in other words, if a man is not a Christian, it is because he is an unbeliever in the fact that, as sure as the Bible is true, there is nothing on earth so profitable as Christianity. 'Godliness,' says the Scripture, 'is profitable unto all things'; and if a man believes in Jesus Christ as a reality – as the Son of God and as the Son of Man, having all power – and as so loving him that He will exercise all His power for his good – that man will love Jesus, and, forsaking all that he has, will go to Him; but a man will care nothing about Jesus unless he believes that 'He is.'

Again. You cannot go to Jesus unless you forsake all that you have. Rebekah had but one choice: to forsake all that she had, or to give up Isaac. It was impossible for her to remain in her father's house, and at the same time go to Canaan. All that she had formerly lived for and delighted in must be renounced and left behind, or she could not become the bride of Abraham's son. And so it is with you. If you would have Christ, your father, your father's house, and the other things in which you have hitherto found your only delight must be given up. By nature the devil is your father, the world your father's house, and the indulgence of the flesh that in which you seek your pleasure. Now you cannot go to Christ unless you resist the devil, crucify the flesh, and come out from

16

the world. It is true in one sense you go to Christ before you commence doing any of these things, and from the moment you do go you are safe. Rebekah may have been considered to have given herself to Isaac from the moment she said, 'I will go,' and from that moment Abraham was pledged to do all in his power to take care of her; but the 'I will go,' of Rebekah implied a determination on her part to renounce all that hindered. It was an absolute necessity indeed that she should, for if she did not, she might promise what she pleased, but she neither could nor would ever go to Isaac.

It is now with you as it was then with her. Rebekah is the type of every sinner who passes from death to life. As she was called on to give up all that she had for Isaac, so are you now called on to give up all that you have for Christ. Every necessary preparation has already been made to ensure you a successful journey, and you have only to say, 'I will go,' and to start in the strength of Him who offers you His Son, and nothing shall be too hard for you, or harm you. The world, the flesh, and the devil will most certainly fight against you; but as your days, so shall your strength be. The way may be long and weary, perhaps grievous, and often painful – sometimes very painful – but the end is certain. Having escaped every danger and overcome every enemy, as Isaac brought Rebekah into his mother's tent, so shall you be brought with gladness and rejoicing into the King's palace. Look not at the cross then, but keep your eye upon the crown. It was for the joy set before Him that Jesus endured the cross and despised the shame; and He sets the same motive before His invited bride. With His own lips He has said – 'To him that overcometh will I grant to sit with me on my throne, even as I also overcame, and am sat down with my Father on his throne.' Wilt thou go with this Man?

17

Lastly. If you accept Christ, remember it is *now* that He offers Himself. You have no security that He will ask you tomorrow, or the next day, or a month hence. He asks you today, and if you accept Him He is yours for ever; but refuse Him today, and tomorrow you may be in hell, or hardened.

I believe that Rebekah's family were thoroughly worldly people. I believe that the sight of the bracelets and the earrings was as weighty a reason as any with Laban for asking Abraham's servant to his house at all (verse 30), and with all their profession of belief that the thing proceeded from the Lord, he and his mother certainly tried to put a hindrance in the way of Rebekah; which our natural relations, the world, the flesh and the devil, have almost always tried to put in the way of every sinner professing to go to Jesus: 'Let the damsel abide with us a few days.' (verse 55).

The faithful servant having told his history and asked the family for their answer, we read, 'Then Laban and Bethuel answered and said, The thing proceedeth from the LORD: we cannot speak unto thee bad or good. Behold, Rebekah is before thee, take her, and go, and let her be thy master's son's wife, as the LORD hath spoken.' This answer fully satisfied the servant, and so we find that when he heard these words 'he worshipped the LORD, bowing himself to the earth.' He then ate and drank, which he had refused to do until he had told his message and got his answer. After that he retired for the night, full of faith in the promise made him. In the morning he rose up, and his first recorded words are, 'Send me away unto my master.'

What then must have been his astonishment when her brother and her mother said, 'Let the damsel abide with us for a few days, at the least ten; after that she shall go'! How earnest, how energetic is his answer: 'Hinder me not, seeing the Lord hath prospered my way; send me away that

I may go to my master.' Reader, I believe there are multitudes now in hell, and multitudes with whom the Holy Spirit will never strive again on earth, who have lost their souls, after having made up their minds to go with Christ, through putting off their departure for *these ten days*. Something once happened to them – no matter what – a sickness, a death, a sermon, a conversation with a godly friend, and God made that something His messenger to convey His offer of Jesus. The offer was thought of, dwelt upon, entertained. The poor sinner, like Laban and Bethuel, was constrained to say, 'The thing proceedeth from the Lord:' he was awed, solemnized; he could not refuse, and he determined that, let him have to give up who or what he might, he would forsake it all, and accept and go with Jesus.

In the moment that determination was made, the Holy Ghost said, '*Now*'; and in the same instant the world, and the things that bind to the world, cried, '*Not now.*' You shall go – you must go – we would not hinder you altogether, but do not go this moment; at least stay long enough to put your worldly affairs in order, and to bid them farewell who are of your father's house. 'Abide with us a few days, at the least ten; after that you shall go.'

Abraham's servant would not listen to such a proposal, neither will God the Spirit. 'Hinder me not' is His cry; and if you will not go with Him *now*, He will leave you where you are, and go without you. If He does, He will go away grieved, and He may never come back again. As Rebekah answered for herself, however, so must you. And your reply must be straightforward – God asks you if you will accept Christ, and the only answer He will receive is 'Yes,' or 'No.' 'And they called Rebekah, and said unto her, Wilt thou go with this man? She said, I will go.' What do you say?

2: The Love of Christ – His Riches

I HAVE COME TO YOU IN THE NAME OF THE LORD JESUS, and I ask you, 'Wilt thou go with this man?' Do not say you will not, until you have heard what I have to say about Him.

Paul says to the Corinthians, 'Ye know the grace of our Lord Jesus Christ, that, though he was rich, yet for your sakes he became poor, that ye through his poverty might be rich.' (2 Cor. 8:9). The Corinthians knew this, but then the Corinthians to whom Paul wrote were converted people; they had been taught by the Holy Ghost to know what no man could either find out or believe for himself – the love of Christ. If you are an unconverted man you know nothing of that grace which led the Lord Jesus, though He was rich, yet for your sake to become poor. Paul had gone amongst the Corinthians, seeking a bride for his Master's Son. He told them of His love; the Holy Ghost blessed the words spoken by Paul, and many of them believed. I will, God helping me, try and tell you what Paul told the Corinthians, and may the same Spirit that taught and blessed him, teach and bless me also.

The grace of God! The love of our Lord Jesus Christ! Wherever he went it was a wonderful tale that Paul had to tell; and from Paul's days to our own, wherever God's messengers go, they have the same to tell. To the neediest, to the poorest, to the most destitute of God's creatures this is their message: *Jesus Christ, though He was rich, for your sakes became poor, that ye through His poverty might be rich.*

I cannot run the risk of letting you pass hurriedly over

this message. It is a message from God to you. Look at it word by word. 'Jesus Christ.' Think who Jesus Christ is. He who in the beginning was with God, and who was God, He by whom all things were made, and without whom nothing was made that was made, He whom the Holy Ghost describes as 'rich – what did He do? He became poor. For what? For your sake: that you through His poverty might be rich.

In the last chapter I dwelt much on faith. I now ask you, Have you faith to believe what you have just read? If you have, it will surely dispose you to love Jesus. Many people are loved for their riches, but it must be true love indeed that makes a person willing to become poor himself that he may enrich the object of his love. Yet this did Jesus, and for your sake. 'Wilt thou go with this Man?'

You know very well what men mean when they speak of poverty and riches, but did you ever consider what God means? Remember, God's thoughts are not as our thoughts, and that which is highly esteemed among men is abomination in His sight. God does not consider a man rich or poor according to the multitude of the earthly things that he possesses. To one who thought himself rich He said, 'Thou art wretched, and miserable, and poor, and blind, and naked' (Rev. 3 : 17); and to another, in the midst of tribulation and earthly poverty, he said 'Thou art rich.' (Rev. 2 : 9). God sees not as man sees. In passing Lazarus at the gate of Dives, how few would have thought that Lazarus was the richer of the two! Yet which was the more truly rich? He who was clothed in purple and fine linen, and fared sumptuously every day, or the beggar that was laid at his gate desiring to be fed with the crumbs that fell from the rich man's table? Doubtless thus put to you, you will answer – the beggar. But do you really believe it? and if you do, what was it that made him richer than

the rich man? There can only be one answer: *he had God.*
He had nothing else: the rich man had everything else.
The rich man had everything except God; Lazarus had
nothing except God. This one possession neutralized the
riches of the one and the poverty of the other. Lazarus has
long since entered into possession of the incorruptible
inheritance to which he was born heir, when he was born
of God the Spirit; while he, who in this world had everything but God, has been begging in vain for centuries, and
must continue to beg in vain for ever, for a drop of water
to cool his tongue.

Carry this with you, not only while you read this book,
but in your estimation of things through life – that he that
has God is rich, and that he that has not God is poor.

The earliest account in Scripture, both of the riches of
Christ and the love of Christ, is, I think, found in the eighth
chapter of the book of Proverbs. In that wonderful passage, from the twenty-second to the thirty-first verse, Christ,
the Wisdom of God, condescends to make known to men
things concerning Himself – things that have been from
everlasting – things which we must receive by faith; for
while they are beyond our natural comprehension, they
are things which He has revealed, and which we may
therefore be sure are as true as the Word of God.

'The Lord possessed me in the beginning of his way,
before his works of old. I was set up from everlasting, from
the beginning, or ever the earth was. When there were no
depths I was brought forth; when there were no fountains
abounding with water. Before the mountains were settled,
before the hills was I brought forth: while as yet He had
not made the earth, nor the fields, nor the highest part of
the dust of the world. When he prepared the heavens I
was there: when he set a compass upon the face of the
depth: when he established the clouds above: when he

strengthened the fountains of the deep: when he gave to the sea his decree, that the waters should not pass his commandment: when he appointed the foundations of the earth: then I was by him, as one brought up with him: and I was daily his delight, rejoicing always before him: rejoicing in the habitable part of his earth; and my delights were with the sons of men.'

You have here a summary from His own mouth, of what were the riches and love of Christ. Let me speak first of His riches. 'From everlasting' – this is something that passes our comprehension. Man can understand in a degree, 'without end,' but he cannot understand 'without beginning.' But from everlasting the Father – Jehovah – God had possessed the Son, and the Son the Father. On the night on which He was betrayed, Jesus Himself addressing the Father, said, 'Thou lovedst me before the foundation of the world.' And so He did. From everlasting, He was *daily his delight, rejoicing always before him.*

Now God Himself has no greater gift to give than the gift of Himself; and the richest man in the world is the man that has the most of God. Who then can conceive what were the riches of Christ? Who then can conceive of what ever had been, and what must ever have been, the complete, and perfect, and impossibly-to-be-increased satisfaction of His every hour and every moment. Never from eternity had there been an instant in which He was not the well-beloved of His Father; never for a moment had He been without God. The Father was with Him always, and the Son was always with the Father; from eternity He had been by Him, as one brought up with Him; daily His delight, and rejoicing always before Him. What could increase the infinite possession of the Son? Surely He had no want. Surely in the highest sense it might be said of Him, 'He was rich.'

But the passage reveals not His riches only but His love. O how shall I speak of that which passes knowledge? God was the only riches of the Son, but not the only object of His love. The Father was the object of His daily delight, but not the only object in which His soul delighted. Notwithstanding His great possessions, there was still a want in the heart of Christ. Even in the presence of the Father there was an unfulfilled desire – a longing vehement going out of affection – His desire was towards an object He could not call His own, and which not even the Father Himself could unconditionally give Him.

I know that I am now speaking of deep and solemn mysteries, for I am speaking of Christ and His Church. While I pray God to set a watch upon my lips, and would be very careful what I write, I do not fear to say, for Scripture says it, and the conduct of the Lord has proved it, that from everlasting another object in conjunction with the Father shared the love of the Son, and possessed His heart; an object, as He afterwards proved, for the sake of which He was willing to come down from heaven, and, though He was rich, to become poor. That object was, *the sons of men.*

O who can understand the height, and depth, and length, and breadth of the revelation made to us in the short passage I have quoted from Proverbs! He whom Paul calls 'the wisdom of God,' (1 Cor. 1 : 24) there reveals to us first of all His uncreated and eternal existence with the Father, from everlasting daily His delight, and rejoicing always before Him. It may be however that this, though it never could have been known without direct revelation to the sons of men, might have been known to angels and archangels, to principalities and powers in high places; but neither angel nor archangel, or any mind that God ever made, could conceive without direct revelation the wonderful truth that follows, that while the Son was the delight

24

of the Father, rejoicing daily before Him, the Son was rejoicing not only in the Father, but also rejoicing in the habitable part of His earth, and His 'delights were with the sons of men.'

Read the passage, I beseech you, if you are not intimately acquainted with it, or if I have not so expressed myself as to be clearly understood. Christ the Wisdom of God, the only-begotten Son of the Father, He who by inheritance was sole Heir to all the treasures of Jehovah, has declared to us with His own lips of truth, that from all eternity, as was the Father's love to Him, so was His love to the fallen sons of men.

On the night on which He was betrayed, Christ said to His disciples, 'As the Father hath loved me, so have I loved you.' They were wonderful words, and I once heard a holy man say that they were harder for him to receive with the faith of a little child than any words in all the Bible; yet Jesus only repeated then what His Spirit had revealed a thousand years before to Solomon.

And now I have to tell of another marvel. The sons of men, the objects of Christ's love and in whom was His delight, were lost, lost to God; so lost that even God Himself could not unconditionally give them to His Son.

By the mere word of His mouth God could make the worlds, but by the mere word of His mouth God *could not give man to Christ*. God made man originally in His own image, but man sold himself to work iniquity in the sight of the Lord, and his sins separated between him and his God. Man after the fall ceased to belong to God; that is, he was no longer God's to deal with as He would. He became Satan's lawful captive, and was only God's to deal with in justice: that justice handed him over to Satan, and Satan alone could deal with him as he would. Satan led him captive *at his will*, and whatever else Satan might do with him,

25

he would never willingly make him over to the sinless Son of God. God was not only lost to man, but man was lost to God; so that as man was without God in the world, God it seemed must be for ever without man in heaven.

All the created wisdom of heaven and hell combined could not discover how even God Himself could bring back man to God. The only-begotten Son of God might love him, and had loved him from eternity, but His love could not deliver him out of the hand of Satan. In the judgment of no created intelligence was it possible that the Son of God and the sons of men could ever meet in love. As it is now in hell, so it seemed to be then on earth – between heaven and earth there was a great gulf fixed, a gulf impassable not to man only, but to God. Man had broken the law of God, and so become debtor to the law; by the law he had been brought before the Judge: the Judge had found him guilty, and delivered him to the executioner, and the executioner had cast him into prison until he should pay that debt; and now the Judge, even God Himself, would cease to be a just Judge, and a just God – or, in other words, cease to be God at all, if *on any plea whatever He brought him out thence until he had paid the uttermost farthing.*

And how fully has the Son proved that, even for the sake of His love, He never would have asked this of the Father! Is there unrighteousness with God? God forbid. Will He deliver the lawful captive unlawfully? God's law was in the heart of the Son, and even His love of man gave way before His hatred of sin. *He could die, but He could not sin for man.* Satan would have given man to Jesus if He would have sinned for him. For a single bow he offered Him the world, but the only reply he got was, *'Get thee behind me, Satan.'* (Luke 4 : 8).

Well did Satan know that this was the one thing that the Son of God would not do for the fallen sons of men, and

26

on this knowledge he felt secure, that as by God's justice they were his, the Son would abide alone, and he should keep his goods in peace. By the law of God they were his property, and cost Him what it might, the Son would 'magnify the law, and make it honourable.' Who then could pluck these lost ones out of Satan's hand? Not even God Himself: for He would cease to be a just God the day He became a Saviour.

Assuming these propositions to be correct, and that the wisdom of all creation could see no further, I would now ask my reader, with all reverence, to draw in his mind's eye a picture of that scene in heaven from which the Lord Himself has been pleased to lift the veil.

In the full sunshine and glory of the Light, which no man can approach unto, stands the Son. At the moment we see Him, He is what He has been from all eternity – daily His Father's delight, and rejoicing always before Him. The heart of the Father is going out towards Him, and in that heart there is but one feeling, 'This is my beloved Son, in whom I am well pleased.'

But where is the heart of the Son? Towards the Father truly: still it is evident that He is not occupied with the Father exclusively and undividedly. The Father is lifting up the full light of His countenance upon Him, but His face is not just now towards the Father; there is in it an earnest, longing, loving look, but it is directed into the distance. His whole attitude is that of one who is gazing on some loved and longed-for, yet very far off, object. We see too between Him and the object on which His gaze is fixed a great gulf – a gulf that seems to every one, even to His love, impassable. Angels and devils know His love, *but all see the gulf,* and do not believe that even His power can bring His loved ones to Himself.

And who is this that is sharing the heart of the Father

with the Son, and yet is so hopelessly separated from Him? Hear, O heavens, and be astonished, O earth, it is those who have rebelled against God – who have destroyed themselves, and become the prey of the mighty – those on whom a sentence of everlasting destruction has been passed; they are Satan's lawful captives, the lost sons of men.

It is eternity! It is a solemn moment in eternity. These two – the Father and the Son – are together there in eternity! The eyes and heart of the Father are on the Son; the Son's delights are with the sons of men. Well do the all-seeing eyes and loving heart of the Father follow the eyes and read the heart of His beloved Son. Suddenly the silence of heaven is broken. A voice proceeds from the excellent glory. The Father speaks, and the Son, who hears Him always, listens. What says God the Father to His only-begotten Son? 'Ask of me, and I shall give thee the heathen for thine inheritance, and the uttermost parts of the earth for thy possession. (Ps 2 : 8).

O the depth of the riches both of the wisdom and knowledge of God! How unsearchable are His judgments, and His ways past finding out! *The one thing* that seemed impossible even for Him to do His wisdom has overcome; and now we know that nothing, *not even the salvation of man*, is impossible with God. He had said, 'Ask of me, and I shall give you.' And it matters not what may be the apparent obstacle, whatever God has once promised we may be quite sure He is able also to perform. This promise was given to the Son, and once given it was certain, if the Son would ask, that the mind of God had devised means by which He could be 'a just God and a Saviour' – means by which He could rescue the sons of men from Satan, and give to the Son of God 'the heathen for His inheritance, and the uttermost parts of the earth for His possession.'

But will the Son ask? The Almighty God is able to make

the offer, but will the Son accept it? In the moment the scheme of redemption was known to the Father it was known to the Son also, for they are one, and have but one mind, and one spirit, and 'the Father sheweth him [the Son] all things that himself doeth.' (John 5 : 20).

Well did the Son know what the gift entailed. It was a gift truly – a free gift – but at the same time a terrible gift for the acceptance of the Son. 'Thine they were,' said Jesus, 'and thou gavest them me.' It was a gift which if accepted entailed works; a gift that must be purchased with the loss of all that He had.

It was a hard trial of love. Will the love of the Son endure the trial? Will He who from eternity had been daily His Father's delight, consent to go forth from before His presence to save the sons of men? Thoroughly does He know to what He must go forth : the agony and the bloody sweat, the cross and passion, the death and burial, are all before Him. No one was ever called on to go forth from, or to go forth to, what He was. Surely He has possessions enough. Surely for these lost ones He will never leave the glory that He has with the Father. So we should think, so all but Himself would think; but He loved the sons of men, and never was there love like unto His love. Many waters could not quench it; love of self could not turn it. It was strong as death, and His face was set as a flint to ask; for if He asks not He must abide alone, and those whom He loves are lost.

He asks. The covenant is entered into, ordered in all things, and sure; and God gives the heathen to His Son for an inheritance, and the uttermost parts of the earth for His possession.

To you, to me, to all is the word of this salvation sent, and there is now an open door for every one of us, by which we may be saved; yet it will not profit if it is not mixed with faith in those that hear it. It is true that as yet we do not see all things put under Jesus, but they will be, for the mouth of the Lord has spoken it; but we see already the fruit of His asking: Satan's captives have become, and are becoming the Lord's freedmen; the heirs of wrath are made the heirs of God, and joint heirs with Christ; and the children of the wicked one, wedded to the world and sin, the children of God, through union with the Lord Jesus. These things we see around us, and they are pledges of the fulfilment of the promise; and these things never could have been unless the Son *had asked*. If He had saved Himself, He would have doomed you and me to everlasting destruction; but He saved not Himself, that He might be able to save us. Wilt thou go with this Man?

If you have not yet decided, hear, before you say you will not, what I have still to tell you.

3: The Love of Christ – His Poverty

IN THE LAST CHAPTER I TRIED TO SHOW WHAT WERE by natural inheritance the riches of Christ. He had God. He was daily His delight, rejoicing always before Him. I endeavoured to point out to you also a little of His love: to show you how from all eternity He had loved the sons of men; so loved them, that until He could call them His, there was to His eye a void even in heaven; so loved them, that, with all their sin and its penalties upon them, He asked them of the Father. Let us now see what this love, this asking, cost Him.

In the last passage that we considered we saw the Son in close communion with the Father. He had received the promise of the heathen for His inheritance, and the uttermost parts of the earth for His possession. What period may have elapsed from then until the time mentioned in the Scripture I am next to bring before you, I know not. One day is with the Lord as a thousand years, and a thousand years as one day, and we are not to seek to be wise above what is written; but it is written: *'When the fulness of the time was come, God sent forth his Son, made of a woman, made under the law, to redeem them that were under the law, that we might receive the adoption of sons.'* (Gal. 4:4, 5).

The words you have just read are 'the true sayings of God.' They are very few, and very simple; yet do they contain the revelation of a salvation which the wisdom of God alone could have conceived, and the love of God alone have executed. In them is declared by the Spirit of God the great mystery of godliness – 'God manifest in the flesh.' Receive them in their plain and literal fulness, believe in them, and rest in them, and they will be life and strength to you; alter them, explain them away, or reject them, and good would it have been for you if you had never been born.

'When the fulness of the time was come' – that is, when the very best and most suitable time for the fulfilment of His promise had arrived – 'God sent forth his Son.'

'God sent forth his Son', the one who had been with Him from eternity, never separated from Him for an instant, daily His delight, rejoicing always before Him. God sent Him forth. Try and conceive not only what must have been the love of the Son to come, but the love of the Father to send Him. I desire in this little book to commend to you the love of Christ, and to speak to you of Him, if peradventure as God prospered the way of Abraham's servant so He may prosper my way, and I may persuade you to go to be bride to my Master's Son; but let no one suppose that I would paint the love of the Father as being one whit less than the love of the Son. God is love, and there is and ever was the same love in the heart of the Father, the Son, and the Holy Spirit – three Persons yet one God – towards the sons of men.

Wonderful things are spoken of the love of the Father. If anything could be more amazing than that the Son in His love should have asked us of the Father, it is that the Father in His love should have given us to the Son. And yet He not only gave us, but I have Scriptural warrant for saying, He was *pleased* to be asked, and *pleased* to give us. And as the Son knew, so the Father knew what the gift entailed, and to what He sent forth His son. Before we could be redeemed from the curse of the law His soul must be made an offering for sin; without this, no child of Adam could be saved; and in this strait 'it pleased the Lord to bruise' not us, but Him. (Isa. 53 : 10). *It pleased Him*. Man was lost to God, and God loved man; yet unless God sent forth His Son to be wounded for our transgressions and bruised for our iniquities, man never could have been brought back to God. Our sins had placed God, if I may so speak, in this position : either to leave us to our deserved fate, or to save us at the expense of His Son. What did He do? 'God so loved the world that he gave his only-begotten Son, that whosoever believeth in him should not perish, but have everlasting life.' God 'spared not his own Son, but delivered him up for us all.' Surely, surely the love of God, as well as the love of Christ, passes knowledge. They are identical – one and the same thing; and he that has seen the Son, has seen the Father also. No one loves us as God loves us; no one loves us like Jesus Christ.

God sent forth His Son – but it was neither to instruct archangels, nor to redeem the angels who kept not their first estate. 'God sent forth his Son, made of a woman.' As had been foretold her by the angel Gabriel (Luke 1 : 26–35), the Holy Ghost had come upon Mary, and the power of the Highest had overshadowed her, and a 'holy thing' was to be born of her; that 'holy thing,' says the angel, 'shall be called the Son of God.' But a body had been prepared Him; the Son of God was 'made of woman,' and his mother 'brought forth her first-born Son, and wrapped him in swaddling clothes, and laid him in a manger, because there was no room for them in the inn.' (Luke 2 : 7). In the fulness of time God sent forth His Son, made of a woman, and *the Son of God became the Son of man!*

Look into the manger at that little helpless infant. Prophets have desired to do it and wise men journeyed far to do it; and if you will not look, prophets and wise men will rise against you in the judgment. Do you recognize the babe that lies there? You have seen Him before. It is the Son of God, He who from all eternity had delighted in the sunshine of His Father's countenance; He who from all eternity had delighted in the sons of men. To what has His love brought Him? Look at Him once more: your heart may soften while you look. You remember what He was; you see what He is. Could He have been richer? Could He become poorer? Look again: all this was for your sake; though He was rich, yet for your sake He became poor, that you through His poverty might be rich. Wilt thou go with this Man?

And what was the after-life of this little Child? Not only was He made man, but 'a Man of sorrows.' Had He been born heir to all the wealth, honour, and earthly comfort the world could give, who even then could express the depths of His poverty when compared with the riches He had with the Father; but for your sake He became not only poor, but poor even amongst the poor of this world. He was hungry, and He had no food; weary and had not where to lay His head. He was tempted, falsely accused, often obliged to flee from place to place to save His life, reviled, buffeted, betrayed, mocked, spat upon, scourged, forsaken, and at last closed a life of pain and sorrow with a death of shame and agony. Add to this that He – the only pure, the only holy, the only sinless Man in the whole world – was doomed to dwell in the midst of ungodliness, and endure the continued contradiction of sinners against Himself – and surely you will acknowledge He did indeed become poor. Never forget why. I cannot repeat it too often – it was for your sake; that you, through His poverty, might be rich.

But the Word tells us not only that He was 'made of a woman,' but 'made under the law.' It tells us the reason, too: 'To redeem them that were under the law, that we might receive the adoption of sons.'

Now it must be remembered that man is not the child of God by nature; by nature no man has a right to call God Father. Man is by nature a sinner, and God never made a sinner. God made man in His own image, perfectly pure and holy, and man has only to look into his own heart, which is enmity against God, to see that he is fallen; that he cannot be what God made him. It was the devil that made man a sinner, and by nature the devil, not God, is the sinner's father. I know this truth is most offensive, but it is true for all that. The Jews said to Jesus, 'We have one Father, even God. Jesus said unto them, If God were your Father ye would love me. . . . Ye are of your father the devil.' (John 8:42–44). And as were the Jews by nature, so are you and I – the children, not of God, but of the devil.

It is because he sinned and so broke the law that man ceased to be the son of God; for that man only has a right to call God Father who can present Him with a life of sinless obedience. But this no man can do, 'for all have sinned, and come short of the glory of God.' Yet the loving heart of Christ yearned to bring man back to God, and longed to call him 'brother, sister;' yea, even by a dearer title – 'spouse.' (Song of Sol. 4:9). And what did He do to accomplish it? He was 'made under the law,' and being made under it, kept it. He magnified it and made it honourable. Made of a woman, He was in all points tempted like as we are, yet when Satan came to Him he found nothing in Him. He was without sin. He came to fulfil the law, and He fulfilled it: not one jot or one tittle passed away until it was fulfilled. He did what no man ever did, or ever could do: worked out for Himself a perfectly pure and sinless righteousness, a righteousness which in virtue of its own merits gave to its possessor a right and title to enter heaven.

You remember the great gulf which once seemed for ever fixed between God and man? This obedience to the law, this righteousness which He wrought out, was one of His wondrous plans for making a way across it by which man could go to God, and God to man; and this righteousness He laid up among His treasures. If you would have God for your Father, you must accept Christ; for it is only by union with His Son that you can become a child of God. But accept Him, and with Himself He will give you this righteousness; and appearing before God in it, you will appear as He does before God, sinless. He was made under the law that He might redeem them that were under the law, that we might receive the adoption of sons.

Wilt thou go with this Man?

4: The Love of Christ – His Poverty

THE SON OF GOD HAS BEEN SENT FORTH BY THE Father, and has become the Son of man. Beyond comprehension is the height from which He has come down; beyond comprehension the depth into which He has descended. As we said before of His riches – truly He was rich; so now we can say of His poverty – truly He has become poor.

Yet poor as He became as the Son of man, the Son of God must become poorer; far far poorer, before He can deliver the lawful captives of Satan, or make a way across the gulf between Him and the sons of men. 'The Lord God and his Spirit' (Is. 48:16) had sent Him forth, and for the sake of His beloved He had been 'made of a woman, made under the law.' He had fulfilled the law under which He was made, magnified it, and made it honourable; and, as man, worked out a perfect and spotless righteousness. Not needing this righteousness Himself, it was His to give to whom He would, and He had wrought it out expressly that He might give it to the sons of men. In His righteousness He knew that the very vilest of His loved ones appearing before God, would for that righteousness' sake be counted righteous also; and He wrought it out as a marriage robe, a wedding garment to have in readiness for His bride – the first gift He would present to her after she had accepted Himself.

But now the wedding garment is ready, where is the bride? Though Christ has righteousness to give, where are those to whom He would give it? In legal bondage! still unredeemed, and so still in Satan's keeping. A gift of righteousness is ready. Christ, having kept the law, had become 'the end of the law for righteousness' (Rom. 10 : 4); but the 'great gulf' still remains, and is apparently as impassable as ever. Sin, unexpiated and unatoned for, is still upon His loved ones; and though a gift of perfect righteousness will give a *presence of righteousness,* it cannot atone for the presence of sin. Sin, and its curse, is on mankind, and until the wages of sin are paid Satan will not give up his captives, nor will the law cease her demand, 'Pay me that thou owest!'

What is to be done? God had said, 'Ask of me, and I shall give thee the heathen'; and the Son had asked. In the fulness of time God had sent forth His Son; and the Son, as man, made under the law, had kept it. In virtue of His own sinless obedience, He had now a righteousness by the gift of which He could make the chief of sinners righteous. It was evident to all who desired to look into these things that the wisdom of God had found means to provide righteousness for the sinful sons of men.

But what avails this righteousness while the guilt of sin is on man? Until that is taken away, God cannot forgive. Man must remain under its curse, and receive its punishment. God must find a way to make the sinner without sin, or He can never take him out of the hands of Satan, and deliver him a freed man to His Son.

And can God do this? Can He find a way to make the sinner sinless? Eternal life or eternal death hang upon the question; for if He cannot, no flesh can be saved. Still, fear not, believe only, and in all boldness answer, Yes; for has He not said, and shall He not do it? If God could not have saved man He never would have promised the heathen to His Son.

There is a way – God has discovered it; but into what depths will it sink the Son! My heart fails, and I tremble while I write it. If He who was made man for the sons of men would also be made sin for them, if Christ will not only give them His righteousness, but take their sins upon Himself – their sins, to bear their guilt, and to suffer their punishment – then, indeed, might the guilty sons of men, putting on Him their garments of sin, be unclothed and freed from sin, and so made free to accept Him, and the righteousness He had wrought out for them. The sins of the sons of men had brought the Son of God to this, that having been made man for them, He must also be made sin, or leave them to perish for ever.

What will He do? Will 'that holy thing,' who was made man, be made sin for the sons of men? He did love us, and His Father loved us: they both loved us dearly, but will Christ for that love be made sin in the sight of God, and will God for our sakes lay sin upon the Son? Let the Holy Spirit answer: 'He hath made him to be sin for us, who knew no sin; that we might be made the righteousness of God in him.' (2 Cor. 5:21).

Christ made man! Christ made sin! Surely He is poor now! I trust you are remembering that this was all for *you*; that He might be able to make *you* the offer of Himself. His being made man passes knowledge; there were lengths and breadths of love in it that no heart but His own could ever know, but His being made sin – oh, it is impossible even to try and speak about it! His being made man for us was as nothing compared to His being made sin.

Think who He was – 'The Lord of Hosts,' 'Your Redeemer,' 'The Holy One of Israel.' (See Isa. 43:14; 44:6). This was His name. And as your Redeemer – God manifest in the flesh – He consented to be made sin that you might be made 'the righteousness of God in him.' Wilt thou go with this Man?

And now, in asking you to go with this Man, I should like you to be very clear about the way in which He is made sin for you, as also about the way in which you can be made 'the righteousness of God in Him;' for a mistake on this point might neutralize His work for you, and leave you in Satan's kingdom for ever.

First you have to receive this as a truth, and it is a truth whether you receive it or not, that if you were judged by the merits of the best act you ever performed, there has been sin enough in it, when tried by the standard of God's law, to condemn you. You never did a single thing in your whole life which in God's sight was not full of sin. Now as you never did an act in your whole life which was righteous in God's sight, so Christ never did a single act which was sinful in God's sight. As the thoughts of your heart have been and are evil, only evil, and that continually, so the thoughts of His heart were holy, only holy, and that continually. The consequence is that the life of man, the best man that ever lived, brings him in guilty before God, but the life of Christ brings him in righteous before God.

Now Christ has no need of this righteous life for Himself, having by natural right an inheritance in the kingdom of heaven; so that He has it as it were amongst His possessions, and is at liberty to give it to whom He pleases. Those for whom He wrought it out were not only free from righteousness, but had been the servants of sin (Rom. 6: 20); and, though the obedience of Christ could supply righteousness, *it could never take away sin.* What was to be done? O, 'kiss the Son' and rejoice with trembling. He covenanted with the Father, not only to work out a righteousness for us, but to bear our sins in His own body. And now He urges us to accept His righteousness, and invites, yea, entreats us to lay our sins upon Him. He loves us, and desires us for His own; and so not only is He willing to take our sins, but we actually grieve His Holy Spirit if we will not lay them on Him; for unless we accept His righteousness, and lay our sins upon Him, we can never be His.

By the grace of God, and under the teaching of His Spirit, a multitude that no man can number have laid their sins on Jesus, and in this way He has been made sin for them. If He is to be made sin for you, you must lay your sins on Him. God never saw a sinner on earth so loaded with sin as Him who did no sin; for, sinless Himself, He 'bare our sins.' 'The Lord hath laid on him the iniquity of us all.' God 'made him to be sin for us who knew no sin, that we might be made the righteousness of God in him.' Without this His obedience would have availed us nothing. Wilt thou go with this Man?

The Son of God has been made man for us. He has been made sin; but is even this all He has to bear before He can redeem us? Surely we have got to the depths of His poverty now; surely He can sink no lower. Even if it were possible, surely His love can endure no further. Such would be the thoughts of every human heart, but how little does the human heart know either of the requirements of the law, or the love of Christ. Having put His hand to the plough, will He look back? Having begun, will He not perfect that which concerns us? He can and does sink lower, and His love can and does endure it.

He has been made sin for us, and sin of necessity brings with it the curse of God. No matter who he is, the man who has got sin on him has got God's curse on him. He who now offers Himself to you, and who bore all this that He might offer Himself – our precious, blessed Saviour, the Man Christ Jesus – was no exception. As long as His beloved ones were in their sins the curse of the law was on them; but when at His invitation they gave themselves to Him, He accepted them, as the bridegroom accepts his bride, and took them just as they were. When He took them He took their sins, and when He took their sins He took their curse.

God sent forth His Son, made of a woman, made under the law, to redeem them that were under the law; and He did that which God sent Him forth to do, and redeemed those God had given Him: but it was by taking not only their sins, but also their curse. Thus says the Lord, by the mouth of Paul, 'Christ hath redeemed us from the curse of the law, being made a curse for us.' (Gal. 3:13).

Wilt thou go with this Man? If you will not, is it not because you do not believe what you are reading? Again I tell you that Christ endured all this that He might offer Himself to you; and having endured it, He does offer Himself. But I also again tell you that it will not profit you unless you receive it into your heart by faith. And if it does not profit you it will harden you, and do you injury past telling: it will not only leave you as it found you, with the curse of God upon you, but if you reject His love, and provoke Him to jealousy, it will bring down upon you 'the wrath of the Lamb.'

Christ made man; Christ made sin; Christ made a curse. Surely salvation is accomplished now! There can be no further humiliation – no deeper depth of poverty into which the Son of man must descend before He can deliver the lawful captive, and set Satan's prisoners free. Again our hearts deceive us if we think so. Christ has yet more to suffer, or the sons of men must remain unsaved.

He has taken our sins, and He who did no sin has the curse of sin upon Him. He has our sins: He has our curse; but He has yet to endure our punishment. Well did the precious Saviour know it. On the night on which He was

42

betrayed He said, 'This that is written must yet be accomplished in me, And he was reckoned among the transgressors' – reckoned not only by man, but by God, and receive *from* both the reward of transgression (Luke 22: 37). On that night He could say, 'The things concerning me have an end.' He had been made in our nature, and, in that nature having fulfilled all righteousness, had taken on Himself our guilt and its curse; but still He had more to bear. Before He could say, 'It is finished,' He must receive 'the wages of sin.'

I am approaching the most solemn and mysterious portion of my subject. While I pray the Holy Spirit to guide me, I will try in what I say to keep as closely as possible to the words of Scripture. We read in John's Gospel that 'Jesus knew that his hour was come' – that hour foretold seven hundred years before by Isaiah, when God should 'make His soul an offering for sin'; and we are then told by Matthew that He went to the garden called Gethsemane. Here He 'began to be sore amazed' – whatever the wonderful expression may be intended to convey to us – 'and to be very heavy.' Here His overcharged and well nigh broken heart sent the confession of His agony to His lips, and He says to His disciples, 'My soul is exceeding sorrowful, even unto death.' Here, showing us how we should act in time of trial, He did not lean on earthly friends or human comforters, but, leaving His disciples at a distance, went alone to His Father. Alone with God He fell on His face, and prayed; and how does His prayer discover both the intensity of His suffering and the perfection of His obedience! 'O my Father, if it be possible let this cup pass from me: nevertheless, not as I will, but as thou wilt.' Here, being in an agony, He prayed yet more earnestly, and His sweat was as it were great drops of blood, falling down to the ground.

I will not try to expatiate, for I shall only weaken the sense. Here He who from all eternity had been daily His Father's delight, rejoicing always before Him, is betrayed by one disciple, and forsaken by the remainder. Then, laid hold of as a common malefactor, He is led away 'to Caiaphas, the high priest, where the scribes and the elders were assembled.' Here He is buffeted, spat upon, smitten, and by Jewish rulers, priests, and people condemned to be guilty of death. By them He is then sent to Pilate, and by Pilate to Herod. Herod, with his men of war, set Him at naught, mock Him, array Him in a gorgeous robe, and send Him again to Pilate. As a lamb before his shearers is dumb, so before Pilate He opens not His mouth. By Pilate, though he acknowledged that he found no fault in Him, He is condemned, scourged, and delivered to be crucified; at that crucifixion He knew all that should befall Him: that at the cross, if He went to it, He must be trodden in the winepress of God's wrath alone.

Hitherto His Father had been with Him always: and in His times of need God had sent His angel from heaven to strengthen the man Christ Jesus; but if He goes to that cross, He must be forsaken not by man only, but by God. He must receive the wages of sin. He could have saved himself: for though it pleased the Father to bruise Him, the Father had put His life in His own power. The Father loved Him because He laid down His life: but He laid it down of Himself: no man took it from Him. At any moment of time He could have prayed to His Father, and He would have given Him more than twelve legions of angels; and surely in that moment of trial, He, who was in all points tempted like as we are, must have been sorely tempted to cry for deliverance. He did not cry, however; and why not? Because if He had, He would have been saved, and if He had been saved, He could not have saved

He was sore amazed

The Love of Christ

you. He was sore amazed, and in an agony; His soul was exceeding sorrowful, even unto death; but there was one sorrow which would have been greater to Him than any He had to bear: and that would have been the sorrow of not being able to offer Himself to you. Will you accept Jesus? Wilt thou go with this Man?

Then Pilate took Jesus, and scourged Him. 'And when he had scourged him, he delivered him to be crucified. Then the soldiers of the governor took Jesus into the common hall, and gathered unto him the whole band of soldiers. And they stripped him and put on him a scarlet robe. And when they had platted a crown of thorns, they put it upon his head, and a reed in his right hand: and they bowed the knee before him and mocked him, saying, Hail, King of the Jews! And they spit upon him, and took the reed, and smote him on the head. And after that they had mocked him, they took the robe off from him, and put His own raiment on him, and led him away to crucify him.' (Matt. 27:26–31).

Reader, 'behold the Lamb of God, which taketh away the sin of the world.' Behold Him by faith, as He goes forth from the hall of Pilate to be crucified for our sins. Too weak to bear the cross Himself, 'as they led him away, they laid hold upon one Simon, a Cyrenian, coming out of the country, and on him they laid the cross, that he might bear it after Jesus. And when they were come to the place which is called Calvary, there they crucified him.' (Luke 23:26, 33).

They crucified Him. 'Christ hath redeemed us from the curse of the law, having been made a curse for us: for it is written, Cursed is every one that hangeth on a tree.' (Gal. 3:13). *They crucified Him.* 'Now from the sixth hour there was darkness over all the land, unto the ninth hour. And about the ninth hour Jesus cried with a loud voice saying,

Eli, Eli, lama sabachthani? that is to say, 'My God, my God, why hast thou forsaken me?' (Matt. 27:45, 46).

'My God, my God, why hast thou forsaken me?' Jesus made man; Jesus made sin; Jesus made a curse; Jesus forsaken of God! That agonizing cry has proclaimed to every created intelligence that there exists not a poorer creature on the earth than the once rich Son of God, the Man Christ Jesus. God Himself can make man no poorer than to leave him without Himself; and behold Jesus for our sins is *without God in the world.* All we can imagine of evil is contained in the words *without God.* It is God's punishment for sin; it is His curse; it is death; it is hell.

It is true that a man may be without God and not feel it; but that matters not. He who never feels it here, will feel it for ever in the world to come, for God has determined that sooner or later every man shall know and feel what it is to be without God. *In the moment that Jesus was without God, He felt it.* As the hart pants for the water brooks, so His soul thirsted after the living God; and therefore before He said, 'It is finished,' He cried, 'I thirst.' Think not it was mere thirst of body that wrung the cry from him. His was the thirst of a bereaved and emptied soul; the thirst of which all God's people know something; the thirst caused by being without God and feeling it; the thirst that has the promise, *It shall be satisfied.* The man who feels it now is 'blessed' (Matt. 5:6), and for him God has in Christ opened rivers of living water. The man who is without God in the world, is the poorest, the most wretched, and the most to be pitied of God's creatures. He abides in death – the death that Adam died in Paradise when he sinned; the death that all Adam's children have died in him; the death that Jesus died for us when He was made a curse for us, and 'himself bare our sins in his own body on the tree.' All the malice of men and devils combined ever failed to wring the slightest murmur from Him, but the wages of sin broke His heart, and in a loud voice, under the hidings of His Father's countenance, the cry burst from Him, 'My God, my God, why hast thou forsaken me.'

I believe that the agony which the lost soul will experience for ever and ever, will be the mysterious agony that wrung that cry from Jesus.

And now there remains no more to be done or suffered. The righteousness of the law has been fulfilled; the penalty of sin has been paid; and as He bows His head, crowned with thorns, on His breast, stained with that blood which cleanses from all sin, and commits His departing spirit into the hands of Him who gave it, the Saviour Himself exclaims, *'It is finished.'*

It is finished! The veil of the temple is rent in twain – the way into the Holiest of all is made manifest; and the great gulf which since Adam's sin had separated between God and man, is no longer a great gulf fixed. Jesus Christ has bridged it over and there is now a way across it by which God and man can pass to one another in love; *that way is by and through Himself.* Though He was rich, yet for your sake He became poor that you through His poverty might be rich. He was brought to your state – 'without God in the world,' that you might be brought to His state – 'daily His Father's delight, and rejoicing always before Him.' God, though He loves the sinner, is of purer eyes than to behold iniquity; and no man on whom is a particle of sin can see God and live. Who then could live in His presence? Who, when all had sinned, could appear before Him without sin? That God and man could ever so meet, at one time was, and seemed as if it must ever be, an impossibility; but when Christ said, *'It is finished,'* the impossibility was no more,

47

and the way was opened. Mercy and truth had met together: righteousness and peace had kissed each other.

Our judge is God Himself: He charges His angels with folly, and in His sight the heavens are not clean; but man can now stand before God, holy and unblameable and unreproveable in His sight (Col. 1:22), for Christ has shed His blood to wash man; He has wrought out Righteousness to clothe man. Washed in His Blood man is cleansed from all sin, and clothed in His Righteousness he is made the righteousness of God in Him.

It is finished! Sinner, you have nothing to do, for Christ has done it all for you. As Rebekah believed the word of the messenger, and went to Isaac, so it is for you to believe the Word of God, and go to Jesus.

Wilt thou go with this Man?

5: The Love of Christ – His Riches

'WHEN THE EVEN WAS COME, THERE CAME A RICH man of Arimathæa, named Joseph, who also himself was Jesus' disciple: He went to Pilate and begged the body of Jesus. Then Pilate commanded the body to be delivered. And when Joseph had taken the body, he wrapped it in a clean linen cloth, and laid it in his own new tomb, which he had hewn out in the rock: and he rolled a great stone to the door of the sepulchre, and departed.

'Now the next day, that followed the day of the preparation, the chief priests and Pharisees came together unto Pilate, saying, Sir, we remember that that deceiver said, while he was yet alive, After three days I will rise again. Command therefore that the sepulchre be made sure until the third day, lest his disciples come by night, and steal him away, and say unto the people, he is risen from the dead: so the last error shall be worse than the first. Pilate said unto them, Ye have a watch: go your way, make it as sure as ye can. So they went, and made the sepulchre sure, sealing the stone, and setting a watch.

'In the end of the Sabbath, as it began to dawn toward the first day of the week, came Mary Magdalene and the other Mary to see the sepulchre. And, behold, there was a great earthquake, for the angel of the Lord descended from heaven, and came and rolled back the stone from the door, and sat upon it. His countenance was like lightning, and his raiment white as snow; and for fear of him the keepers did shake, and became as dead men. And the angel answered and said unto the women, Fear not ye: for I know that ye seek Jesus, which was crucified. He is not here: for he is risen, as he said. Come, see the place where the Lord lay. And go quickly, and tell his disciples that he is risen from the dead.' (Matt. 27 : 57–28 : 7).

He is risen! O what a glorious Scripture is Romans 7 : 4! When, through the finished work of Christ, the Holy Spirit was enabled to declare to us this word of God, the Lord Jesus saw of the travail of His soul, and was satisfied. I have often considered the passage as an epitome and condensation of the whole Gospel; an embodiment of the resurrection cry of the Saviour; the full utterance of what from eternity His loving heart had longed to procure and to proclaim – yet which He could never have either procured or proclaimed, if He had not purchased the power with His own blood. Do you know the passage? Listen to it! 'Ye are become dead to the law by the body of Christ; that ye should be married to another, even to him who is raised from the dead, that we should bring forth fruit unto God.'

Marvellous, yet faithful saying – hard to flesh and blood to receive, yet worthy of all acceptation! Each and every sinner, even the chief, born under the law, accepting Christ becomes dead to the law. Such is the proclamation, with the graciously-vouchsafed explanation, 'Ye are dead to the law by the body of Christ.'

By the body of Christ! Take great notice of the words, for having brought yourself by your own sins under the curse of the law, they teach you the only way by which you can be delivered. You can never become dead to the law by repentance, or amendment of life, or any other thing that you can do. By what you have already done you have lost your soul; but by nothing that you can ever do can you redeem it. In spite of every endeavour the law will demand it; for to redeem a soul costs a ransom that of yourself you can never pay. But you can become dead to the law so that, though you have broken it, it shall have no power over you to condemn you – 'by the body of Christ.'

But you ask, What does this mean? Before I try to tell you, lift up your heart to God, and pray that for Jesus Christ's sake He will give you His Holy Spirit to open your eyes. Have you done so? Now try and see *by faith* a cross, and hanging on that cross *a body*. Remember, I do not tell you to get a picture or a crucifix, for it is expressly commanded that, on no pretence whatever, should we make a likeness of anything that is in heaven or earth, for the purpose of religious worship; but I tell you, after prayer to God, to try and see that cross and that body *by faith*. Do you see them? do you recognize them? That cross is the accursed tree on which our Saviour bore our sins, and that *body is the body of the Lord Jesus!*

But how comes that body there? What hand of sin and sacrilege has nailed it to that cross? That body is there as an atonement for your sins. It was the sins of His people that nailed Him to that cross. Never lose sight of that dead body – never take your eyes off it, until by faith you can say, He was wounded for my transgressions, He was bruised for my iniquities; though my sins were red like scarlet, they are become white like snow; though guilty, I am pardoned and saved. I am dead to the law by the body of Christ.

If you have faith in Christ you are dead to the law; and if you are dead to the law you are pardoned and saved, for you are freed from the law as a covenant. You are no longer held by it in legal bondage; no longer tied and bound to it in the letter which kills. Are you dead to it? Are you free? Are you pardoned and saved? If you are a believer in Jesus, I say again you are, and you only dishonour Him if you fear to say you are.

And now, who made you free? Christ! Christ made

51

man, Christ made sin, Christ made a curse, Christ forsaken of God, Christ hanging a dead body on the accursed tree, has made you, by this total surrender of Himself, dead to the law – free. And why did He do this? Why, with such utter disregard of self, did He sacrifice Himself to free you from the law? I have called this passage our Lord's resurrection cry – let it answer my question: 'Ye are dead to the law by the body of Christ; that ye might be married to another, even to him who is raised from the dead, *that we might bring forth fruit unto God.*' At such a cost to Himself, Christ freed the sinner, that the sinner, being free, He might make him the offer of Himself. Wilt thou go with this Man?

There is no such thing as a barren union with Christ. It is the universal characteristic of His true people that *they bring forth fruit unto God*.

He is risen! What the angel commanded the women to tell to the disciples, Christ Himself has commanded His disciples in all ages to tell to everybody. I tell it to you: 'Christ is risen.' He who, in love to the sons of men, took the burden of their sins upon Himself, and was cast into prison until He should pay that great debt, has paid it to the uttermost farthing. By His death in our stead He has made a full, perfect and sufficient sacrifice, satisfaction, and oblation for the sins of the whole world. Both the demands of the law and the justice of God have been met and satisfied, and Christ is now able to save to the uttermost all them that go to God by Him. The proof is, 'He is risen.' He went to the cross covered with sin. God made Him to be sin who knew no sin, by laying upon Him the iniquity of us all. No man, as I said before, was ever so laden with sin as the Man Christ Jesus. No man ever had so much sin to answer for; but He has answered for it all, and it is on Him no longer; He has put it away by the sacrifice of Himself; He has washed it away in His own blood. He was cast into prison until He should pay that great debt; the proof that He has paid it is, that He is out of prison – 'He is risen.'

He was crucified, dead, and buried; He descended into hell; but the third day He rose again. The agony and the bloody sweat, the cross and passion, the death and burial – all are over; and Christ is risen to ascend up where He was before, 'now to appear in the presence of God for us.' (Heb. 9:24).

If Christ were not risen, Christians would be of all men most miserable; we should yet be in our sins. But now is Christ risen, having spoiled principalities and powers. Now is Christ risen, a victor over death and the grave. O death, where is thy sting? O grave, where is thy victory?

Christ came forth from His Father and His God, and for our sakes became poor; but He has risen not only to ascend again to His Father and His God, but to ascend to Him even richer than before. He is risen, and He will ascend to His Father, taking with Him what He had not before; He will ascend, taking with Him *the riches of His grace*.

The riches of His grace! O what an addition even to the riches of Christ! Had He not these amongst His treasures, the riches that He had with the Father before the worlds were could have profited man nothing; had He not gone down into the depths we have been considering there could have been no way, as I said before, for God to come to man in love. But now has Christ both lived and died, and risen again; now has He endured the curse, and paid the penalty; now having triumphed over His enemies and ours, now having spoiled principalities, and powers, and spiritual wickedness in high places, He will ascend up on high, leading captivity captive, to receive gifts for men, yea even for the rebellious, that the Lord God may dwell among them. (Ps. 68:18). He will ascend, carrying with Him His 'portion' (Deut. 32:9), 'His peculiar treasure' (Ps. 135:4) – a multitude that were lost, but are now His redeemed and saved people – a multitude, once heirs of hell, but now heirs of God and joint heirs with Christ – a multitude whom He is not ashamed to call brother, sister, spouse – 'The church of God, which he hath purchased with his own blood.' (Acts 20:28).

Many times after His resurrection, before He ascended to Him who was now not only His Father, but their Father, did He show Himself to His disciples. When the time came that He should be received up, He led them out as far as Bethany. And He said unto them, Go ye into all the world and preach the Gospel to every creature. And he lifted up His hands and blessed them. And it came to pass while He blessed them, He was parted from them, and carried up into heaven.

The Lord was manifested to destroy the works of the devil, and the Lord hath gotten Himself the victory. 'Lift up your heads, O ye gates; and be ye lift up, ye everlasting doors; and the King of glory shall come in. Who is this King of glory? The Lord strong and mighty, the Lord mighty in battle. Lift up your heads, O ye gates; even lift them up, ye everlasting doors; and the King of glory shall come in. Who is this King of glory? The Lord of Hosts, He is the King of glory.' (Ps. 24:7–10).

'Now that he ascended, what is it but that he also descended first into the lower parts of the earth? He that descended is the same also that ascended up far above all heavens, that he might fill all things.' (Eph. 4:9, 10). 'It is Christ that died, yea rather, that is risen again, who is even at the right hand of God, who also maketh intercession for us. (Rom. 8:34). 'He was delivered for our offences, and was raised again for our justification.' (Rom. 4:25).

Wilt thou go with this Man?

6: Paul at Rome seeking a Bride for his Master's Son: the sort of people to whom he went

DO YOU REMEMBER WHAT I TOLD YOU WAS THE ONE thing necessary to be believed by Rebekah, before she would for a moment feel even an interest in the proposition made by Abraham's servant? It was absolutely necessary that she should believe there really was such a person as Isaac.

Now have you carried this much faith with you through the history you have been reading? Do you really believe that there is such a Person as Jesus Christ; and that He, the Son of God, was made man, sin, a curse for your sake; that to save you He refused to save Himself, but endured the punishment of your iniquity, and so opened a way for your redemption? Do you really believe that now having endured the curse, and received the punishment your sins deserved, He actually and truly offers you *Himself*? Whether you believe it or not, nothing can be more literally true, and nothing but unbelief on your part can separate between you. God grant that you may feed on Him in your heart by faith, and thankfully accept Him.

O what joy filled the heart of the risen Saviour, as He gave the commandment to His disciples, 'Go ye into all the world, and preach the Gospel to every creature.' It was for this joy that He endured the cross and despised the shame; it was for this He came down from heaven. He had a baptism to be baptized with – it was a baptism of blood – and how was He straitened until it was accomplished; but the baptism of blood, and the cross, and the shame are over, and He is about to ascend up where He was before. His power to give this commandment, 'Go ye into all the world, and preach the Gospel to every creature,' was the power for which He lived and died and rose again.

The Gospel! Do you know what it is? Glad tidings of salvation through union with Jesus. All the world had broken the law, all the world was lying in the wicked one (1 John 5:19); but go ye, says Jesus, to every captive of Satan – to all that are under the law, to all whose sins have condemned them to eternal death, to every creature on this side of the grave – and ask them to come to me. Tell them that I can save to the uttermost, and that I cast out none; nay more, tell them that I have loved the sons of men with an everlasting love, that I have died to save them, that I have risen again; and that now, 'just and having salvation,' through my own finished work, I am free to offer myself to them, and they are free to accept me. Tell them what the Son of God, the Man Christ Jesus has done for them, and then ask them from me, Wilt thou go with this Man?

In obedience to this command the disciples went every where preaching the Gospel. Rare in those days was the instance of a man who, really united to Jesus, was not stirred up to be a living epistle, known and read of all men. If he did not address multitudes, for which perhaps he was not fitted, yet in season and out of season he preached Jesus by his conduct, and as he had opportunity also in conversation. Not only the Spirit, but the Bride said 'Come,' and every one that had the gift of utterance stirred up the gift that was in him. The preaching and teaching of some of the early disciples has mercifully been handed down to us. Let me select that of the Apostle Paul, a holy man of God, who spake as he was moved by the Holy Ghost. I have already said, at the beginning of this book, that this man went among the Corinthians, seeking a bride for his Master's Son. Now we know that as Eliezer of Damascus was sent forth by Abraham, so Paul was chosen and sent forth by God, and that being infallibly guided, not only was what he said precisely that which God would have had him say, but those to whom he went were precisely those to whom God would have had him go, and are exact specimens of those to whom in all ages His messengers should go.

Let us take first his Epistle to the Romans. We have there a description written by himself of the sort of people to whom he went. Surely we shall see a picture of all that is amiable and excellent on the earth. As you look at it, drawn by his own hand, remember that he is painting the objects of Christ's love – those who from all eternity had been daily His delight, those with whom He desired to enter into a marriage covenant, that they might be with Him where He was, and as one with Himself share His glory, and abide with Him for ever.

Truly in their state, as Paul went to them, they were to the eyes of men not very lovable. But God does not see as man sees. Paul describes them as 'filled with all unrighteousness, fornication, wickedness, covetousness, maliciousness; full of envy, murder, debate, deceit, malignity; whisperers, backbiters, haters of God, despiteful, proud, boasters, inventors of evil things, disobedient to parents, without understanding, covenant-breakers, without natural affection, implacable, unmerciful: who knowing the judgment of God, that they which commit such things are worthy of death, not only do the same, but have pleasure in them that do them.' (Rom. 1 : 29–32). These, and such as these, we learn from Paul himself, were the sort of people amongst whom he went seeking a bride for his Master's Son.

Now I believe that it would be very difficult to find a

man who would choose for his bride one who, by her outward life, left it a matter of no doubt that she was guilty of many of the iniquities here mentioned, and harder still to find a man who would acknowledge that he himself was full of them. Yet I speak it fearlessly when I say that in this long catalogue of twenty-three sins, there are only two, murder and fornication, that are not committed openly every day; committed not only by the glaringly, unblushingly immoral, but by the respected and respectable; by their children, too, of both sexes and all ages; by high and low, rich and poor, young and old together; and that not only without fear of God, or remembrance that these sins are damning, but without sense of shame, or loss of worldly character.

Now the passage that contains the catalogue of these sins is the Word of God, and tells us that, *in the judgment of God,* they who do such things are worthy of death. But though man knows this is God's judgment, his own judgment differs from God's, and he believes what he thinks, and not what God says. It is true that man forms his own laws to some extent according to God's laws; if he did not, society would be unbearable. Man only altogether neglects those commandments that have reference to his duty towards God. These anyone is at liberty to break with impunity; but it is not so with the commandments that relate to man's dealings with his fellows. Were the last six commandments of the law as little attended to as are the first four, neither life nor property would be safe, and for the great mass of mankind the earth would not be habitable. I can imagine no greater approach to a hell upon earth than that man should treat the commandments which teach him his duty towards man as he treats those that teach him his duty towards God. But man is aware of this, and requires that just so much of the outward and gross ugliness of sin shall be restrained as would spoil his enjoyment of this present world.

Society in society always pretends to love its neighbour as itself, and however flagrantly this law may be broken elsewhere, it is never suffered to be broken there. Any sin against God may be committed in society, if it is not at the same time a sin against society. The world's morality is: Sin must be kept down and restrained when it is injurious to society, but the world need interfere with it no farther. I believe the most popular man with the world will be the man who contrives most flagrantly to break God's laws without offending against the laws of society.

Now in so far as their development would offend against the well-being of society, I am willing to admit that the sins mentioned by Paul are more or less forbidden by the world, but not one jot beyond that. As it was in his days, so it is in ours – though men know that in the judgment of God they who do such things are worthy of death, they 'not only do the same, but have pleasure in them that do them.' O surely we have need to pray, 'From all hardness of heart, and contempt of Thy word and commandment, good Lord deliver us.'!

I should like to look at this list of sins in detail. First we have the general term 'wickedness.' Do men really think what God considers 'wickedness' a great sin?

Forgetfulness of God, the not having God in all one's thoughts, is the essence of all wickedness; yet I believe that this sin is so little thought of that multitudes of people who call themselves Christians would rather be thought God-forgetting than vulgar. I believe, also, that multitudes of parents would prefer that their son should have the character of being the wickedest, rather than the stupidest boy in his school. I believe that many parents would feel proud of a son of whom the master said, 'He is one of the cleverest boys I have, but I am afraid he never thinks of God or his soul,' or at least would be more satisfied than if they were told, 'Your boy is a very good boy. I have really no fault to find with him; but I am sorry to be obliged to add that he is very stupid; he seems to understand or care for little except his Bible.'

Be honest, reader. Which would you prefer? – for yourself, that you should be thought God-forgetting or vulgar? for your child, that he should have the character of being a wicked boy or a stupid one? After you have thought over this question, and honestly answered it, then remember this: that while God tells us on the one hand that not many mighty, not many noble, not many learned are called, but that He chooses His people from the weak, and the base, and the despised of this world (1 Cor. 1:27), He tells us, on the other hand, that 'the wicked shall be turned into hell, and all the nations that forget God.' (Psalm 9:17).

'Covetousness' is next mentioned. In the judgment of God the covetous man is worthy of death. Yet, is this sin uncommon? or is the man whose heart is exercised with covetous practices thought the worse of by the world? The word 'abhorreth' is a strong word, and, so far as I know, only occurs five times in the Bible. Yet on one of these occasions it has been used by the Holy Spirit to tell us that God abhorreth the covetous man. But does that affect him in the estimation of the world? Alas, no! No matter what God thinks of him, only let him add house to house, and field to field, and the wicked will bless him; and the more he prospers in his covetousness, the more he will be sought after, and courted, and flattered. It is with him now just what it was when David wrote, some three thousand years ago: 'The wicked boasteth of his heart's desire, and blesseth the covetous, whom the Lord abhorreth.' (Ps. 10:3).

'Maliciousness, envy, debate, deceit, malignity, whisperers, backbiters, haters of God, despiteful, proud, boasters, inventors of evil things': are not some of these things inmates of your heart, as well as of the hearts of those about whom Paul wrote, and does not the conduct and conversation of many, in whose society you take pleasure, prove that they are in their hearts also? Yet does the world think worse of you, or you of them that do such things? The seeds of all these sins are in you and in everybody, and if you are sufficiently interested in the matter to watch yourself, you can soon discover their fruit. Some may show in a lesser, some in a greater degree, but these are the things that are in the heart, and come out of the heart of every natural man; and the man who does not curb them, and *because they are sinful* struggle to root them out, is in the judgment of God *worthy of death.* You cannot deny this – you dare not, in the very face of God's Word before you. Yet how uncharitable does it seem to that man whose maliciousness, envy, deceit, and such like develops itself to no greater degree than an average development, and whose hatred of God shows itself to no greater extent than an average hatred – that is, in habitual forgetfulness of religion, so long as it is not forced on him, and only in active enmity when it is what he calls crammed down his throat – how uncharitable, I say, does such a man think you, when you tell him that the wrath of God abides on him; that because he does these things, and chooses his companions from those who do these things, in the judgment of God he deserves everlasting death! Yet *it is* the judgment of God; and men know it, while they deny it. They know that the Bible says that these things are the works of the flesh, and that if we live after the flesh we shall die; but though they know it, they do not really believe it. The hearts of men and the teaching of God's Word are in opposition, and men believe their own hearts more than God's people, God's Word, or God Himself. They sin against God, yet they fear not. The devil says to them what he said to our first parents, 'Ye shall not surely die;' and under the power of the devil's lie, the decent, moral, respectable committer of these sins, though he knows in the judgment of God he is worthy of death, will ask you, when spoken to about his soul, what is the great wickedness of which he has been guilty, that you think it necessary to speak to him? Oh, it is fearful to hear such a man tell you, with a countenance that makes you fear he really believes what he says, that though he has not been altogether what he ought, yet God is very merciful, and he cannot see that he has done anything for which He would think him bad enough to put him into hell. Let such a man know that if he habitually gives way to any one of the sins mentioned, no matter how trifling that sin may seem to him, in the judgment of God he is worthy of death; and if he dies without forsaking it, and washing it out in the blood of Jesus, as sure as God is true, He will execute that judgment upon him. What God means by death is ever-lasting damnation.

'Disobedient to parents, without understanding, covenant-breakers, without natural affection, implacable, unmerciful.' These six conclude the catalogue of the twenty-three sins mentioned by Paul in this passage; and though doubtless the natural man, looking at them in their broad literality, will say such things ought not to be, yet will he commit them as it pleases him, to the extent that will not injure him with society, and then stoutly deny, if you press it home upon him, that he has done anything worthy of death.

To honour our father and mother is as much the commandment of God as, 'Thou shalt not steal;' and he who is disobedient to his parents is as much a transgressor of

God's law as he who commits murder. 'Sin is the transgression of the law;' and Paul, writing of himself, says – 'I had not known sin but by the law: for I had not known lust, except the law had said, Thou shalt not covet.' (Rom. 7 : 7). But the law did say, 'Thou shalt not covet;' and Paul did covet. I do not know how often, but at least he did it *once* by his own confession; and in the moment that he coveted, in the moment that with a discontented spirit he wished for some other portion or some other lot than God had given him, in the judgment of God – yes, and in his own judgment also, for Paul was taught of God – *he had done things worthy of death*. And let us remember that when in the judgment of God a man is said to have done things worthy of death, it does not mean that, though God knows he deserves death, He will not inflict death but will let the sinner go free. 'The soul that sinneth it shall die,' says God; and the man who in God's judgment has done things worthy of death, must die; and Paul did die. That one sin, even if he had never committed another, had slain him as much as Adam's one sin slew him; from that moment, however sinless his future life might be, his own life could never stand in the judgment; though he should have to receive for no more, yet he would have to receive the wages of that sin, and 'the wages of sin is death.' (Rom. 6 : 23). For that one sin, had not Jesus died for him, Paul's after-life of devotion could have been no atonement, and he must have spent eternity in hell. It was not his repentance and amendment, but the blood of Christ that saved Paul.

'Without understanding.' Perhaps in the whole list of these sins there is not one at which the natural man would be inclined more boldly to point his finger, and say, 'Surely God does not mean that the man who is "without understanding" is worthy of everlasting punishment.' Yet this is only because 'the natural man receiveth not the things of the Spirit of God: for they are foolishness unto him: neither can he know them, because they are spiritually discerned.' (1 Cor. 2:14). The natural man, that is, a man under the teaching of his own natural heart, would say that to be 'without understanding' was not his own fault, and consequently could not be his sin; that he did not make his own intellect, and so could not justly be made accountable for its deficiency; that let God call man to account for what He might, He never could say that he was worthy of death, and so put him to death for no other reason but only because he was 'without understanding.'

Not knowing the Scriptures, or the power of God, thou dost greatly err, O man, whosoever thou art that would reason thus. 'Cease,' as God tells you, 'from thine own wisdom,' and 'Lean not to thine own understanding.' I doubt whether there is one of the sins mentioned in the long catalogue we are considering, the guilt of which a man more directly brings upon himself, or for the commission of which he is more directly answerable to God, than for the sin of being 'without understanding.'

The understanding spoken of is not natural understanding, but *spiritual*, and no man has it by nature. Many men have by nature a great deal of the wisdom of this world; but no man has, by nature, a particle of the wisdom which is from above. By nature we are the veriest fools in spiritual things; and so long as in them we take our own understanding for our guide, we dishonour God, and do things worthy of death. But though we are 'without understanding,' by nature, it is both our fault and our sin if we remain without it. 'If any of you lack wisdom,' says the Scripture, 'let him ask of God, and it shall be given him.' (Jas. 1:5). And the promise (Prov. 2:3) is positive; 'If thou criest after knowledge and liftest up thy voice for understanding, if thou

seekest her as silver, and searchest for her as for hid treasures, then shalt thou understand the fear of the Lord, and
find the knowledge of God.'

Not to know God, God Himself tells us, is 'to your
shame'. (1 Cor. 15:34). All who do not know Him will be
'punished with everlasting destruction.' (2 Thess. 1:8, 9).

To be *without understanding,'* is to be without excuse
before God, and the very fact that a man is without it
proves that he is careless about God and his own soul.

Show me a man who has been guilty of almost any of
the other sins Paul mentions and it is possible you may
show me a man who, like David, has been led away by
temptation, and fallen into sin; but show me a man who is
'without understanding,' and I will show you a man who
is 'without God in the world;' a man of whom it has never
been witnessed in heaven, 'Behold he prayeth;' a man who
has never been born again of the Spirit; a man who, if he
dies as he is, in the judgment of God has done things
worthy of death, and who will never enter the kingdom of
heaven.

7: Paul at Rome seeking a Bride for his Master's Son: what he said to them

ALTHOUGH YOU MAY NOT HAVE GONE WITH ME IN all that I have said in the last chapter you will agree with me in this: that the people amongst whom Paul went to seek a bride for his Master's Son were people who in the judgment of God had done things worthy of death. Paul himself was most anxious that this should be thoroughly understood; and he occupies not only the first, but the second, and the first twenty verses of the third chapter of his Epistle to the Romans, to prove to the people that he and they – Apostles as others – Jews and Gentiles – each and everybody – were all under sin. He himself asks the startling question, 'Are we,' the Apostles 'better,' in God's sight, than men 'whose damnation is just?' and then sets the question at rest by the reply – 'No, in no wise.' (Rom. 3:8, 9). The law says, 'There is none righteous, no not one;' and 'what things soever the law saith, it saith to them who are under the law: that every mouth may be stopped, and all the world may become guilty before God.' (Rom. 3:19).

And why was Paul thus anxious to prove that all the world was guilty before God? Because God would have all men to be saved, and is not willing that any should perish; and God will save no man who does not acknowledge himself a guilty, and consequently a lost sinner. If you ask me what constitutes a lost sinner, I answer: *to have once broken in thought, word, or deed, any one of God's commandments.* That one sin has for ever destroyed your own righteousness, and brought you under the curse of the broken law; you have destroyed yourself, and are a lost sinner. They who seek a bride for Christ have no authority to seek her anywhere but amongst the lost; for He Himself has expressly told us that He did not come to call the righteous. What He came from heaven to do was to seek the lost; what He came from heaven to suffer was to save the lost; and as the name of the whole family of the redeemed in heaven and earth is *'Christian,'* so the name of the whole family before redemption is *'lost sinner.'* Before union with Christ, 'lost sinner'; after union with Christ, 'sinner saved by grace.'

For this reason it was then that Paul was so anxious to shut everybody up to the fact that they were by nature and practice lost; and for this same reason I am also anxious to shut you up to it. Only acknowledge yourself a lost sinner, and what Paul said to the lost sinners at Rome, I have God's authority to say to you; but until you know that you are lost you will care neither for Christ nor for His salvation.

Let us now see what Paul said to the people at Rome. The doctrines contained in his Epistle are doubtless the same as those he taught when he dwelt amongst them in his own hired house, receiving all that came to him, 'preaching the kingdom of God, and teaching those things which concern the Lord Jesus Christ.' (Acts 28:30, 31).

Imagine him then now surrounded by a multitude of anxious sinners. They have listened to his doctrine about all the world being guilty before God, and have been convinced of sin. They are now persuaded that whatever may be their own judgment about themselves or one another, in the judgment of God they are worthy of death; that all their righteousnesses are as filthy rags, and their sins a burden too heavy for them to bear. One all-absorbing thought is occupying the hearts of a multitude in that company, and that thought is: 'What shall I do to be saved.'

Paul speaks. 'By the deeds of the law there shall no flesh be justified in [God's] sight: for by the law is the knowledge of sin. But now the righteousness of God without the law is manifested, being witnessed by the law and the prophets; even the righteousness of God which is by faith of Jesus Christ unto all and upon all them that believe: for there is no difference: for all have sinned, and come short of the glory of God; being justified freely by his grace through the redemption that is in Christ Jesus: whom God hath set forth to be a propitiation through faith in his blood, to declare his righteousness for the remission of sins that are past through the forbearance of God; to declare, I say, at this time his righteousness: that he might be just, and the justifier of him which believeth in Jesus.' (Rom. 3:20–26).

O the light, and then the delight and joy and peace that rushed in quick succession into the hearts of these poor sinners, as by degrees they received and understood, and by the grace of God believed the words spoken by Paul. They had already received that of which he reminds them at first – that by the deeds of the law (that is, by their own good conduct or righteousness) none of them could be saved; but surely now he is telling them of another righteousness, of another way of salvation. He says, 'But now the righteousness of God without the law is manifested.' What can this mean? It seems as if he intended to teach that *now* there is some way revealed by which a man who has broken God's law, and so lost the righteousness which he ought to have had by keeping the law, may yet get righteousness – perfect, spotless righteousness; a righteousness so perfect, so spotless, that Paul calls it the righteousness of God. If this be so, it is great news indeed;

glad tidings of great joy. But can it be true? Yes, for Paul proves it from the Bible: 'being witnessed by the law and the prophets.' Paul proves from Scripture that he is only teaching what Moses and the prophets, and all the Old Testament writers had universally taught – that salvation was not to be obtained by works of righteousness which we had done, but by the righteousness of which he was then speaking, 'even the righteousness of God which is by faith of Jesus Christ.'

To those amongst his hearers who judged spiritual things by their natural senses, what folly did this doctrine seem! Did Paul mean to say that a righteousness, called in Scripture 'the righteousness of God,' had been manifested, and was now to be offered to every creature; and that this righteousness was not to be worked or laboured for, but accepted as a gift? Yes! Paul evidently teaches that man has no part in working out the righteousness of which he is speaking: for he is speaking of a righteousness 'without the law.' Christ was made *sin* to obtain this righteousness for sinners. 'God made Him to be sin for us who knew no sin, that we might be made the righteousness of God in Him,' and Paul in his preaching to the Romans teaches that man has to accept this righteousness, not labour for it.

But I hear some ask, Who may have it? Who is welcome to it?

The verses I have taken from this Epistle are very full of teaching, and the clause that follows the one I quoted last gives to anxious souls in all ages a plain but complete answer to this most momentous question: this righteousness is 'unto all, and upon all *them that believe.*' By faith of Jesus Christ, he that believes not only may have this righteousness, but *has* it; and then, as if to silence every objector, Paul adds, 'for there is no difference: for all have sinned, and come short of the glory of God.'

No *difference!* No difference between one sinner and another as regards the offer made to them of the gift of this righteousness. Ah, cries the evil heart of unbelief, who can believe this? In my case that never can be true. I have been the chief of sinners. If all the world have sinned and come short, what have not I done? I have doubly and trebly sinned, and come far shorter than them all; surely such a very wicked person as I have been can never be made in God's sight, 'the righteousness of God'! To all such we would again repeat the words of Paul: 'There is no difference.' No difference between one man and another, as to the way in which he must get righteousness; for all have lost their own righteousness, 'all have sinned, and come short of the glory of God.' The amount of sin makes 'no difference.' Out of Christ, he who calls himself the least of sinners must perish; in Christ, the very vilest is made 'the righteousness of God.' If you will take Christ and accept His righteousness, He will accept you, and take your sins.

Surely, my reader, if you have not heard it so often that you are Gospel hardened, the glad tidings Paul proclaims must fill you, as doubtless they did the hearts of many of his Roman hearers, with wondering joy and love. His proclamation is: Pardon and a gift of righteousness for the chief of sinners, and none excluded; no difference between one sinner and another.

But Paul is speaking still, and I would not interrupt him. He is explaining how this blessed state of things has been brought about, namely, because men and women under this dispensation of 'the gift of righteousness,' are not being justified before God, either in whole or in part, by their own works, but are 'being justified freely by His grace through the redemption that is in Christ Jesus.'

Grasp the meaning of what Paul says, I beseech you.

Do not hurry over this most precious truth. God can now justify the sinner who has not one good work of his own to plead; but He can only justify him in one way, that is, 'freely by his grace, through the redemption that is in Christ Jesus.' I have already told you something of what it cost Jesus to purchase this redemption. You have seen Him made man, made sin, made a curse, forsaken of God, to purchase it; but He has purchased it: and now it is *in Him.* Out of Him there is no redemption; no man can redeem either his brother's or his own soul. None but God can justify, and even God Himself only through the redemption which is in Christ Jesus. Refuse Christ, and you must remain unjustified, and consequently unsanctified and unsaved for ever; but take Him, and with Him you get wisdom, righteousness, sanctification, and redemption; God, by His grace and for His sake, will justify you freely. Wilt thou go with this Man?

But Paul does not stop even here. He enlarges, unfolding more completely 'the redemption which is in Christ Jesus.' 'Christ Jesus,' he says, 'whom God hath set forth to be a propitiation, through faith in his blood.' Christ has propitiated God for sinners. Surely no sinner will say, let his sins be what they may, that the propitiation Christ has made is not sufficient to satisfy the demands of God's justice, even for his sins. Remember it was by the sacrifice of *Himself* that Christ propitiated God for sinners; and God having accepted the propitiation, of which He has given assurance unto all men, in that He has raised Him from the dead, has set Him forth as the propitiation for sin, 'through faith in His blood.'

John, in his Epistle dedicated to Christians generally, teaches this doctrine exactly as Paul taught it to the Romans. 'If any man sin, we have an advocate with the

Father, Jesus Christ the righteous: and he is the propitiation for our sins: and not for ours only, but also for the sins of the whole world.' (1 John 2:1–2). So that by this Apostle, as well as Paul, and indeed by all the Apostles, as well as Moses and the prophets, we are taught 'there is no difference,' that 'whosoever will' (Rev. 22:17) – you – I – all and everybody and anybody in the whole world, is invited to go to God in the name of Jesus, and plead with God the blood of Jesus as the propitiation for his sins; and he who so goes, with faith in this blood, has the promise that God will accept him, and for the sake of this blood, forgive him.

'The preaching of the cross,' says Paul in another place (1 Cor. 1:18), 'is to them that perish foolishness;' and what I am putting before you, and what Paul put before the Romans, are the doctrines to which he alluded when he spoke of 'the preaching of the cross.' To some they seemed foolishness in his day, and today may seem foolishness to you. If so, remember to whom it is that God says they seem foolishness. 'To them that perish.' And let them seem to you what they may, the truth will remain the same – that these doctrines are the Gospel of Jesus Christ, 'the power of God unto salvation to every one that believeth.' (Rom. 1:16). Add to, or take from them, and you do it at the risk that God will blot your name out of the Book of Life, and add to you all the plagues recorded in the Bible. (Rev. 22:18, 19). God has set forth Jesus Christ to be a propitiation for sin, through faith in His blood. If, for any reason whatever, man does not believe in the power of this blood in his particular case, but believes in the power of his sins to destroy him – according to his faith it shall be done unto him: *his sins will destroy him;* but if, making God the truth, and giving the lie to his own heart, and every other person or thing that contradicts God's Word, he believes in the redemption that is in Christ Jesus, and has faith in His blood – though he be the most hell-deserving sinner on this side of the grave – the blood of Jesus Christ, God's Son, can and will cleanse him from all sin.

To a man who believes in Christ Jesus, and has faith in His blood, God commands all His messengers to offer, not only forgiveness, but immediate forgiveness; and Paul preaches this doctrine also, in his address to the Romans.

The words following those I last quoted are very strong, and full of teaching, yet are they very simple, and easy to be understood: 'God hath set forth His Son,' says Paul, 'to be a propitiation, through faith in His blood, to declare his righteousness for the remission of sins that are past, through the forbearance of God.'

Now what does this mean? It means that no matter what your past sins have been, you are to do what God tells you to do in 2 Peter 3:15: 'Account that the long-suffering of our Lord is salvation' – account that as God has had such forbearance with you, as not before now to have appointed you your portion with the transgressors, He will not now do it, if you turn to Him. In His name, and by His commandment, says Paul, I preach to you 'the remission of sins that are past.' No matter whether they were committed years ago, or only a minute ago, I offer you, in God's name remission of past sin through faith in the blood and righteousness of Jesus Christ. O it is a wonderful offer for any man to have authority to make; but lest there should be any mistake as to when this pardon might be believed in, and this righteousness accepted, Paul repeats what he had just said over again, in the sentence that follows, 'to declare His righteousness,' and then adds these blessedly clear and unmistakably easy to be understood words, 'at this time.' 'To declare, I say, at this time his righteousness.' What could Paul, or God by the mouth of Paul, say more?

Paul concludes by telling the Romans in fourteen words the object that God had in the whole matter: 'That he might be just, and the justifier of him which believeth in Jesus.'

O the depths of the love, as well as the depths of the wisdom of God! Why could He not have contented Himself with remaining *'just,'* without troubling Himself, especially at such a price, to become *'the Justifier'* of sinners? He has Himself told us why: because He loved us with an everlasting love; because we were the objects of His daily delight from all eternity.

These are the 'good tidings of great joy', which the angel announced to the shepherds when Christ was born, and which Christ before His ascension commanded to be preached to all people. Now, at this time, at this very moment, if you will accept Jesus, God is willing to forgive you all your sins: for in Him He can, while completely honouring His law, which you have broken, be *a just God, and yet your justifier.*

And now let me ask you again: Will you not accept Him? Will you not go with this Man? Remember what He has done only to be enabled to make you the offer. The Holy Ghost would never have inspired Paul to write his Epistle to the Romans, if the Holy Ghost had not had Jesus and His blood and righteousness to reveal to the children of men. Indeed there could have been no Holy Ghost to guide and teach upon the earth at all, if Christ had not received Him from the Father, as the purchase of His own blood. Christ had God, and man had not God, as I said to you in the beginning of this book; so it must have remained for ever, but for Jesus; but for Him, man must have been for ever what Jesus became on the cross – *without God.* But the stipulated reward of His mediatorial work was that God the Father would give God the Holy

Ghost to God the Son, that God the Son might give Him to the sons of men.

And now He has finished the work that His Father had given Him to do and He has received the promise of the Father, and has shed forth the Holy Ghost, who has received of the things that are Jesus Christ's, to show them to us. He showed them to Peter and the Apostles at the day of Pentecost; and during the time they were on the earth He never ceased to show them; and I believe He is showing them still. He showed them to Paul, the day the scales fell from his eyes, and during the time he was on earth He never ceased to show him; and I believe He is showing him still. And from the days of the Apostles unto this our own day, God, for Christ's sake, has ever given the Holy Spirit to them that ask Him. Oh, if you have not yet accepted Jesus, will you not ask God to give you the Holy Spirit! He is the gift of Christ's love, and when He is come He will open your eyes, as He has opened the eyes of all saved people, to see Jesus; and if once your eyes are opened to see Jesus, you will at once accept Him. Man is blind so that he cannot see Jesus until his eyes are opened by the Holy Spirit; but the man who once sees Him always takes Him, for He is the Chief among ten thousand, and altogether lovely. Nothing but blindness keeps men from accepting Jesus. Contemplate Him by faith; think over what you have read about Him, even in this book, even the noble unselfishness of His self-denying love. He commends His love to us, that while we were yet sinners Christ died for the ungodly. It was by dying for His enemies, yet the objects of His love, that He made all things ready for Paul to go to the Romans, and for me to come to you. What say you? Wilt thou go with this Man? It is God who asks you, and again I remind you, the only possible answer is, 'Yes,' or 'No.' Refuse, as perhaps you have too often done already, and again you will

75

grieve His Holy Spirit, and trample on His love; but if, knowing and believing His love to you, you are constrained to answer as Rebekah did, and say, 'I will go,' there will be joy in heaven over your union with Jesus, and in so far as you are concerned, Christ will see of the travail of His soul, and be satisfied.

Wilt thou go with this Man?

8: Paul at Corinth seeking a Bride for his Master's Son

NOTWITHSTANDING WHAT PAUL HAS PREACHED about 'no difference,' and the comments I have tried to make upon his preaching, it is possible there may even yet be among my readers some who think their own case hopeless, because the sins of which their consciences accuse them are so much greater than most of those quoted from the Romans. I will therefore now follow Paul to Corinth, to see what sort of people he went among there, when seeking a bride for his Master's Son.

It is quite true that it is God's object to conclude all men under sin, to stop every mouth, and bring in all the world guilty before Him; but it is for this reason: that He may have mercy upon all. No matter how loathsome and abominable they may have been, there are few things more rejoice God's Holy Spirit than to hear the breathings of a contrite heart mourning over and confessing its sins. God delights in mercy. There is nothing in which He delights so much as to say to a sinner, 'Go in peace: thy sins are forgiven thee.' Yet can He not show that mercy in which He delights, until the sinner feels himself a sinner, and acknowledges his sins. His own Word declares that 'he that covereth his sins shall not prosper; but whoso confesseth and forsaketh them shall have mercy.' (Prov. 28:13). And again: 'If we say that we have no sin, we deceive ourselves, and the truth is not in us; but if we confess our sins, he is faithful and just to forgive us our sins, and to cleanse us from all unrighteousness.' (1 John 1:8, 9).

The publicans and the harlots go into the kingdom of

heaven before the scribes and pharisees, said Jesus; but this was not because the scribes and pharisees were not as welcome to the kingdom of heaven as the publicans and harlots. Jesus would have as gladly welcomed one as the other; but the publican was more easily brought to see his need of Jesus than the pharisee. In reality, there was no difference; both had sinned and come short, and he who comes short of the kingdom of heaven has no portion but the kingdom of hell. But the well-conducted, moral, and strictly-living pharisee, careful of all the outward observances and ceremonies of his church, could not so easily see as could the publican that he had done things worthy of death. The publican, if made anxious about his soul, knew at once that his own conduct had destroyed him and that for a man who had no goodness to set off against his badness, Jesus and His salvation was just suited to his necessity. But it was hard for a man who had fasted twice in the week, given tithes of all he possessed, and after the strictest sect of the law lived a pharisee, to renounce all that enabled him to thank God he was not as other men, and lie at the feet of Jesus on a level with the publican. Yet for both pharisee and publican there is no other way of salvation. Let the worst on earth accept it, and he will be saved; let the best on earth reject it for any other, and he must perish for ever.

I am inclined to think that it is to illustrate and prove this doctrine, that the Holy Spirit guided Paul to give, in his description of the Corinthian sinners, a list of sins so widely different in character from the majority of those I quoted from his Epistle to the Romans. I know perfectly well that the Romans were guilty of sins quite as gross as the Corinthians, but those I have mentioned are recorded in addition. By that list, I believe the pharisee, who would have remained unmoved under the grosser catalogue, must be convinced of sin, and know in his conscience as he reads it, that in the judgment of God he has done things worthy of death; but if there was no other list, the publican and chief of sinners might turn from it in despair, saying, that not only were his sins too bad to be forgiven, but even for God to mention.

But God has, in His mercy, knocked from under our feet every such excuse for unbelief; and in the list He has given of the washed, justified, sanctified, and saved sinners at Corinth, shown us how true is the doctrine that 'there is no difference,' that He 'willeth not the death of a sinner,' but 'will have all men to be saved, and to come unto the knowledge of the truth.' (1 Tim. 2 : 4). The list I have given from the Romans, if judged on the whole by the world's standard, is a tolerably moral and respectable list; but that from the Corinthians tells of sins so utterly and loathsomely degrading that had not the Holy Spirit Himself seen fit to record them for our learning, I should have shrank from their rehearsal.

'Know ye not,' says Paul, 'that the unrighteous shall not inherit the kingdom of God? Be not deceived; neither fornicators, nor idolaters, nor adulterers, nor effeminate, nor abusers of themselves with mankind, nor thieves, nor covetous, nor drunkards, nor revilers, nor extortioners, shall inherit the kingdom of God. And such were some of you.' (1 Cor. 6 : 9–11).

Such were some of you! Such were some of the specimens of fallen humanity, amongst whom Paul was led by the Holy Spirit to seek a bride for his Master's Son. Sinners so degraded, so sunk beneath the level of the very brutes that perish, that it is a mere waste of time to say that you, O reader, would not sit in the room with any one you thought could even tolerate them. I only quote the passage to show how literally true it is that there is 'no difference;'

that as surely as the envious and deceitful man, the proud and the unmerciful, must – unless he forsakes his sins, and accepts God's salvation – perish; so the very chiefest of these Corinthian sinners needed to do nothing more to be saved. The question is not the amount of sin, but whether or not we will accept Christ. Vile as these Corinthians were, Paul had gone amongst them, preaching the Gospel, and asking, 'Wilt thou go with this Man?' and by the grace of God, many had said, 'I will go.' It is in writing to these afterwards that he gives this catalogue of their sins, and concludes the very verse which he begins with the not pleasant but faithful statement: 'Such were some of you,' with an assurance of their full forgiveness. 'Such were some of you; but ye are washed, but ye are sanctified, but ye are justified, in the name of the Lord Jesus, and by the Spirit of our God.' Surely, surely none need despair.

The history handed down to us of Paul's visit to Corinth is full of interest and instruction. On his arrival there, he found a Jew, by name Aquila, by trade a tentmaker. With him he took up his abode; and that he might not be burdensome to any, wrought with him at his trade. Whether he ate, or whether he drank, Paul always endeavoured to do all to the glory of God; and I have no doubt that one of the most useful sermons he preached at Corinth, was the silent sermon of his conduct as he sat working at his craft in the workshop of Aquila.

He began his public ministrations in the synagogue, persuading the Jews and the Greeks every Sabbath-day, and 'testifying to the Jews that Jesus was Christ.' But the Jews would not receive him; they opposed themselves, and blasphemed, so we read that 'he shook his raiment, and said unto them, Your blood be upon your own heads; I am clean: from henceforth I will go unto the Gentiles.' (Acts 18:1–6).

Now remember that these Jews were professed worshippers of the true God, and professed believers in His written word; while these Gentiles, for whom Paul left them, were idolaters, to whom God was an unknown God, and who were living in sins too abominable for repetition. The lesson here taught us is clearly this: *that the Gospel is more likely to be the power of God unto salvation to the vilest sinner, sunk in all the abominations of the Corinthians, than to the respectable and moral opposer of the doctrines that Paul preached.*

I know that what I say is offensive in the extreme. But why? Simply because the soul-destroying conduct of these learned, and respected and respectable Jews, is the exact reflection of the conduct of multitudes of the learned, and respected and respectable amongst ourselves. Should we make the most diligent search, I scarcely believe we could find an individual in the nation who would be guilty of the sins of the Corinthians; yet well do we know that it would be easy to find, especially amongst the mighty and the noble, and the talented in the land, very, very many – oh, how far too many – who would oppose, and who do oppose the doctrines that are taught by Paul.

Paul preaches the doctrine of imputed righteousness, saying, 'As by one man's disobedience many were made sinners, so by the obedience of one shall many be made righteous.' (Rom. 5 : 19). Paul preaches the doctrine of salvation by the blood of Christ, saying, 'Justified by his blood;' 'redemption through his blood;' 'made nigh by his blood;' and 'without shedding of blood is no remission.' (Rom. 5 : 9; Eph. 1 : 7; 2 : 13; Heb. 9 : 22.) Yet who can deny that much of the earthly learning and wisdom of the world is arrayed in open hostility against these doctrines of God – opposing and blaspheming.

Oh, the condemnation such are bringing on themselves!

81

When Jesus sent His disciples to preach the Gospel, He taught them, saying, 'Whosoever shall not receive you, nor hear your words, when ye depart out of that house or city, shake off the dust of your feet. Verily I say unto you, It shall be more tolerable for the land of Sodom and Gomorrha in the day of judgment, than for that city.' (Matt. 10:14, 15). Now Sodom and Gomorrha were destroyed for their gross immorality; yet as sure as these words of Christ are true, it will be more tolerable for the inhabitants of those cities in the judgment than for the man who hears the Gospel and rejects it. Christ says this, and I believe Him. Do you? I believe that if the Corinthian Jew died in his opposition to Paul, and the Corinthian Gentile in his abominable wickedness, that it would be more tolerable for the abominable Gentile than for the opposing Jew.

The drunkard, the swearer, the liar, and all openly immoral and wicked people, have no inheritance in the kingdom of God and of Christ, if they die as they are. It would have been good for them if they had never been born, for God says that they 'have their part in the lake which burneth with fire and brimstone.' (Rev. 21:8). But I am decidedly of the opinion, and I doubt not that I have Scripture warranty for what I say, that the man whom God looks upon as His greatest enemy in this world, and who will be condemned to His sorest condemnation in the next, is the man who, hearing and knowing the great doctrines of the Gospel, disbelieves and opposes them. The murderer has his portion in hell-fire; yet I would rather stand in the judgment as some of the murderers who have been hanged lately, than as the author of some of the books that have been written lately. The one has destroyed one body – the others are doing their best to destroy many souls.

Many of the Corinthian sinners to whom Paul went, answered his question 'Wilt thou go with this man?' as

Rebekah answered it, and said, 'I will go,' and were washed, sanctified, and justified; but how? Paul tells us it was 'in the name of the Lord Jesus, and by the Spirit of our God.' There is no other way of justification; there is no other way of sanctification; and he who contradicts the doctrine of justification in the name of the Lord Jesus, and sanctification by His Holy Spirit, opposes the only name, and rejects the only way given among men whereby we must be saved. That man, continuing in his opposition, can never himself be washed, justified, or sanctified, and consequently can never be saved. (Acts 4 : 12).

The Gospel was offered to the opposing Jew; but for all that the wrath and curse of God remained upon him. The only effect of Paul's preaching was to leave him harder than it found him. And why? For the very same reason, as I have told you again and again in this book, that it may harden you – because he did not believe in it; *it was not mixed with faith in him that heard it.* Instead of receiving the Gospel like little children, the Corinthian Jews began first by reasoning, then contradicting, then opposing, and then blaspheming; till at last their hearts were hardened, and the means of grace were taken from them. It was their own fault – their blood was upon their own heads.

But who can picture the transforming effects of the Gospel on the Corinthians who by faith received it. You know what they were. I have copied Paul's description in his first Epistle; he describes them again in his second, and I will copy that description also. Remember, Paul neither exaggerates nor flatters, but calls persons and things exactly by their right names. He did not hesitate to put these people in mind of precisely what they had been; and now he speaks of them as precisely what they are. The names he gives them in his second Epistle, describe as truly what they became, as did the names in his first describe truly what they had been. No sooner did they accept Christ, than he said to them, 'Ye are washed, ye are sanctified, ye are justified.' But as if these were light expressions to convey an idea of the high estate to which as believers they had been raised, when exhorting them in his second Epistle to walk worthy of their calling, he writes thus: 'I am jealous over you with godly jealousy: for I have espoused you to one husband, that I may present you as a chaste virgin to Christ.' (2 Cor. 11:2).

O, dear reader, who can describe the height and depth, the length and breadth of the metamorphosis that had taken place in these Corinthians? Verily God can bring a clean thing out of an unclean. Remember what they were; look at what they are. But a little while ago covered with unforgiven sin, and accursed of God, and a curse to one another, these people were living in the practice of the most revolting wickedness; but now, not only are they washed, justified, sanctified, but Paul is jealous over them with a godly jealousy because he has espoused them, he says, to one husband, that he may present them as a chaste virgin unto Christ!

If it was not so written, who would dare to use this language? But these are not the words of Paul, but the words of the Holy Ghost. Oh, may He who dictated them to Paul help us to reflect on them. Again I say, think what these Corinthians were; again I say, look what they became, through faith in the offer made them. Not only in that moment were they without spot, or wrinkle, or any such thing, but in the sight of God, and God Himself being the Judge, *chaste enough, pure enough, holy enough to be presented as a bride to His Son.* The blood of Jesus Christ, God's Son, had cleansed them from all sin. The best robe, the marriage garment, the robe of righteousness was upon them: and washed in this blood, and clothed in this righteousness, Christ could say to them, and did say to them, 'Behold, thou art fair, my love; behold, thou art fair.' (Song of Sol. 1 : 15.) The Son could rejoice, and did rejoice over the bride He had won; and the Father could rejoice, and did rejoice to see the bride that had accepted His Son.

Whenever the eye of God fell on the self-righteous opposer of the Gospel at Corinth, the light of His countenance was instantly turned away from him; for God is of purer eyes than to behold iniquity : and that man's iniquity was still upon him, because he rejected Jesus. But one of the greatest delights God ever had upon the earth was in contemplating these justified and sanctified Corinthians. From the moment they said, 'I will go with Jesus,' they were not only never out of His mind, but never out of His sight. Never again was His eye off them. They had become His, for they were united to His Son : they were to Him as the Lamb's wife, the purchase of His blood; members of His body. They were His children, and from that moment He dealt with them as a father deals with his children. He guided them, He taught them, He fed them with food convenient for them; He even corrected them when they needed it. Many a time they did not understand His dealings, for He led them, as Abraham's servant did Rebekah, by a way that they knew not; but all His leadings were in love, and from the moment they said, 'I will go,' He never left them nor forsook them: *long since they have all appeared before Him in glory.*

Reader, it shall be the same with you if you will go with this Man. I wonder if you yet believe that all this is true, and that there is such a Person as Jesus Christ. Remember that God sees everybody either as He saw the unbelieving Jews or believing Corinthians. There is no middle class, and well would it be if men would receive this truth. But receive it or not, it is so; and the person who is not a child of God is a child of the devil.

How important to you then is the question, *Whose are you?* When God looks at you, does He see a believing, or an unbelieving sinner? While your eye is upon this question, His eye is upon you, and no matter what your Christianity may have cost you, are you not repaid for it all at this moment if you can say that, by the grace of God He sees a believer? But if you cannot say so, do you not wish that you could? Do you think sin has ever given you the pleasure that it would give you to know that all the past was blotted out, and that when God looked at you He saw you as He saw these justified Corinthians?

Think what He does see when He looks at you. Nothing is concealed from Him; He knows your past and present; you are naked and open to Him with whom you have to do. God is greater than your heart, and knows all that you know. But if your heart condemns you just now, do not dwell long on this. You are not happy; look away from yourself, and think what He sees when His eyes rest upon His justified and sanctified people. He sees that which is to Him the most lovable and beloved object under heaven – a people without iniquity or perverseness, without spot or wrinkle, or any such thing, a people who, through the finished work of Jesus, are pure, spotless, perfect. They lack nothing, and are complete in Him. As He looks at them, He takes pleasure in them; He delights in them. Of all the things that His hands have made there is nothing like them. They are His own workmanship – not His creation work, but His redemption work. They fell from what He made them at creation, until they were too loathsome for Him to look at; but He has created them anew in Christ Jesus. He now sees, not the Corinthian sinner, but a clean thing brought out of an unclean; a chaste virgin, the fairest work His hands have ever made; a being so chaste, so pure, so holy, that she is chaste enough, pure enough, holy enough to be presented as a bride to His Son.

Do you not wish that when the eye of God rested on you He saw you as He sees His people? And why should it not be so? Let not unbelief stand between you and God. In one moment the great reality of all these great and real things may be your own. The Jesus that I preach to you is the Jesus that Paul preached to the Corinthians; and He is the same, yesterday, today, and for ever. Accept Him under my teaching, as they accepted Him under Paul's, and the Holy Ghost bids me to say to you exactly what Paul said to them. Be your sins past what they may, accept Christ, and in that moment you are washed, justified, sanctified; and what Paul was to the Corinthians, so shall I be to you – the honoured instrument in God's hands of espousing you to one Husband, that I may present you as a chaste virgin unto Christ.

Reader, 'Wilt thou go with this Man?' It will delight the heart of God if you say, 'I will go.' It will grieve His Spirit if you say you will not. I ask you again, 'Wilt thou go with this Man?'

9: Wilt thou go with this Man?

WHAT A WONDERFUL METAMORPHOSIS: THESE Corinthian sinners, washed, sanctified, justified – these slaves of Satan become the children of God, espoused to one Husband, that they might be presented as a chaste virgin unto Christ!

And this had been effected by preaching – or rather by simple faith in the Word preached. These people heard the Word of God, and believed it; and believing, their abominable sins were all washed away, and they became the children of God by faith in Christ Jesus.

In all ages, it has pleased God by the foolishness of preaching, to save them that believe. Woe to them who despise preaching! Paul went to Corinth, and preached Christ crucified. 'I determined not to know anything among you,' he said, 'but Jesus Christ and Him crucified.' To some his preaching was 'a stumbling block,' to others, 'foolishness,' but to as many as believed, both Jews and Greeks, 'Christ crucified' was 'the power of God unto salvation.' (See 1 Cor. 1:24).

Going to preach to such people as these Corinthians, and working such a work as he worked among them, we feel naturally inclined to inquire how Paul began his ministry. Thanks be to God, we have been left in no doubt about the matter. Paul tells us himself in very plain and unmistakable language, exactly how he began. 'I delivered unto you,' he says, 'first of all that which I also received, how that Christ died for our sins.' (I Cor. 15:3).

Now it is impossible to conceive how any two classes of sins could be more opposite in their nature than those committed by Paul the persecutor, the blasphemer, the injurious opponent of Christ and His Gospel, and those committed by these Corinthians; yet the truth that Paul preached to them was the first that he himself received: 'Christ died for our sins.' The fact is remarkable, in that it evidently teaches that for the self-righteous pharisee who verily thought he ought to do many things contrary to the name of Jesus, and for the abominable Corinthian wallowing in uncleanness and sunk below the brutes that perish, there is but one saving truth – 'Christ died for our sins.' It was because both he and they had received this truth that Paul was able to say of himself, 'I obtained mercy'; and of them, 'I have espoused you to one husband, that I may present you as a chaste virgin to Christ.'

I ask you who poison your minds with the trashy and often immoral publications of the present day, when did fiction ever paint such a love-story as this true story of the love of Christ? Cunningly devised fables tell us how heroes have delivered enchanted princesses, risking their lives in combat with giants and monsters; and history tells of kings and princes who have gone in disguise amongst their subjects, better to acquaint themselves with their characters, and to learn better how to serve them; but what writer of romance or history ever conceived, in the wildest dream of his imagination, such a history of love as the history of the love of Jesus! He by whom all things were made, and without whom nothing was made that was made, made Himself of no reputation, and took upon Him the form of a servant, and was made in the likeness of men, and became obedient unto death, even the death of the cross, that He might redeem and win for His bride the utterly degraded and willing captives of that old serpent the devil.

I say again, who, in the wildest dream of his imagination, ever conceived such a love as this? Yet God did this for love. Think who God is. Now then, remembering who He is, remember this is the story of His love. He saw man in his pollution, and lying in his blood. He saw him in his degradation and willing captivity, and *He saw the end of that captivity.* There was no eye to pity, no arm to save. Then, said *He,* 'Lo, I come.' – to save to the uttermost, and supply every need of man. 'Lo I come,' to cleanse the filthy, to clothe the naked, and to anoint the needy with my Holy Spirit. I will prepare the wherewithal to cleanse; I will prepare the wherewithal to clothe, and your anointing shall be of me, says the Lord. And all this, O my people, because I have entered into a covenant with thee; and when I entered into that covenant, *thou becamest mine.* That covenant was of myself, made in Christ, and with Christ, and by Christ, before the foundation of the world; and that not for any foreseen merit in thee above thy fellows, but only and simply because I loved thee, and chose thee. 'I have loved thee with an everlasting love, therefore with lovingkindness have I drawn thee,' or, as it is in the margin, 'have I extended lovingkindness unto thee.' (Jer. 31:3).

This I believe to be God's own account of His own love. He loved His people *because He loved them,* and not because they were a better people than any other. Let those who dispute this doctrine say: Were these Corinthians objects of God's love, loved by Him, and chosen for their goodness? Very clear and full is the teaching of Scripture as regards this. It was when man was lying in his low and lost estate that God said unto him, *'Live.'* 'When I passed by thee, and saw thee polluted in thine own blood, I said unto thee when thou wast in thy blood, *Live;* yea, I said unto thee when thou wast in thy blood, *Live.* (Ezek. 16:6).

What could be more loathsome than the state of the beloved, when He who loved her, said unto her, *Live*? Yet how strong must have been the love that drew forth that word from the lips of God the Saviour. To say it, was to consign *Himself* to death, for the life He gave must be purchased with his own blood. Yet there was no hesitation in His love; He gave unto us everlasting life, and *a body* was prepared Him, in which He might lay down His life as a ransom for the life He gave: 'I delivered unto you, first of all that which I also received, how that Christ died for our sins.' Reader, 'Wilt thou go with this Man?'

Let me here transcribe a translation of an old Latin inscription, which was once given me by a dear friend, and which I then copied into a blank leaf in my Bible.

For the servant, the Master
For the guilty, the Innocent
For the debtor, the Creditor
For the sick, the Physician
For the flock, the Shepherd
For the subject, the King
For the soldier, the Leader
For the work, the Maker
For man, God manifest in the flesh

What shall the servant, the guilty, the debtor, the sick, the subject, the soldier, the man, render? *Let him love.*

With the exception of this story of Jesus of Nazareth, I know of no well authenticated history that tells us of a man laying down his life from the pure and unselfish desire to benefit the object of his love. I do not say such a thing has not been, for peradventure for a good man some would even dare to die, but 'God commandeth his love toward us, in that while we were yet sinners, Christ died for us.' (Rom. 5:8). He died for us, not because we loved Him, but because He loved us; not because He had our love, but to gain it. Now He pleads: Love me, because I first loved you, and laid down my life for your sake. Wilt thou not go with this Man? Think how unchanging His love has been; the same yesterday, today, and for ever. Mercy and goodness have followed you all the days of your life, and only give yourself to Him, and they shall follow you through eternity. Never yet did He leave or lose one that gave himself to Him. Take Him – and as it was said of His disciples, so shall it be said of you – 'Having loved His own which were in the world, He loved them unto the end.' Nothing ever could quench His love, nothing ever will quench it. He bore the wrath and curse of God that it might be preached to every creature; and no creature ever yet believed in it and accepted Him, who was afterwards separated from His love. Paul, the chief of sinners, believed in it, and accepted Him; and after about twenty-five years of experience, what does he say? 'I am persuaded that neither death, nor life, nor angels, nor principalities, nor powers, nor things present, nor things to come, nor height, nor depth, nor any other creature, shall be able to separate us from the love of God, which is in Christ Jesus our Lord.' (Rom. 8 : 38, 39).

Death, with its fears and terrors, was before Paul when he wrote this; and he knew it. It is also before you. Fear not, but be persuaded as Paul was, and *go with this Man.*

Life, with its trials and temptations, was before Paul when he wrote this; and he knew it. It is also before you. Fear not, but be persuaded as Paul was, and *go with this Man.*

Angels, principalities, and powers of darkness, were all leagued against Paul when he wrote this, and had been from the moment he accepted Jesus; and as surely as you take Jesus, they will be leagued against you. Yet, though Paul had been in conflict with these for years, and had the prospect of years of conflict still before him, he says, 'I

am persuaded.' You say the same. Fear not, but be persuaded as Paul was, and *go with this Man.*

You have gloomy views of things present. If it was not
for things present, you say you would take Christ. No
matter what things present may be, they are God's order-
ing. No matter what things present may call on you to
sacrifice, it is God's call. Fear not for yourself; fear not for
your family. Be persuaded as Paul was, and *go with this
Man.*

But it is not the things present, it is the things to come.
I could accept Christ, you say, just now, but when tribulation or persecution arises for the Word's sake, and I am
tried and tempted as I know I shall be, I feel that I shall
fall away, and it would be better for me to make no profession, than to profess and fall away. Brother, accept
Christ, and God is able to make all grace abound towards
you, and to keep you from falling. (2 Cor. 9:8, and Jude
24). Have faith in God, and fear not. *Be persuaded, as Paul
was, and go with this Man.*

Finally, there is no height of distance between you and
God – no depth of sin into which you can possibly have
sunk – no creature in you or out of you, whether in heaven,
earth, or hell, that shall be able to separate you from the
love of God which is in Christ Jesus, if you will only receive
by faith what Paul preached to the Corinthians – 'Christ
died for our sins,' – and *go with this Man.*

10: How Rich you might be!

WILT THOU GO WITH THIS MAN? I AM APPROACHING
the end of my little book, and perhaps you have not yet
said 'I will go.' If so, excuse me for again pressing on you
the question, Do you believe the offer made to you to be
a real one? I cannot understand any one who does, rejecting it. I once more ask, Are you persuaded with anything
approaching to a realizing certainty, that the invisible
person, Jesus Christ, is positively existent; that the story of
His love is a true story; and that when He asks you, as He
does now through me, to forsake your father's house and
all that you have, and enter into a marriage covenant with
Himself, it is as real and true an offer as if made to you by
a fellow-creature? If you believe it, and now start to go
with this Man, as sure as *God is,* the time will arrive when
you will see Him for yourself – see Him as He is. The time
will arrive when in the presence of assembled worlds, the
King in His beauty will acknowledge you as His chosen
and beloved, and, as the daughter of the King of kings and
bride of the Lamb, cause you to sit down with Him on
His throne. If you will go with this Man, all this will prove
itself to be as real and true as God is real and true; but I
remind you again, as I have so often done before, the Word
preached will not profit you, unless it is mixed with faith
in you who hear it. I so often repeat this, because I fear
it may not be mixed with faith *in you.*

But there is another thing besides unbelief that will do
all it can to prevent you from saying, 'I will go with this
Man.' It is the love of the things in your father's house. If

it was not for what you must give up, you say, you would go.

Now think what the love of Christ induced Him to give up for you: to give up, that He might be enabled even to make you an offer of Himself, and put you in a position to accept Him. You know something about it. 'Though He was rich, yet for your sakes He became poor.' You know *something* of how poor. Let me ask you first to think how poor He became for you. It may soften your heart a little, and make you willing to give up something for Him. And think secondly, of the comparative value between what you are called upon to give up and what to accept. 'What shall it profit a man if he gain the whole world and lose his own soul?'

Surely you have faith enough to believe that Jesus, who is the Wisdom of God, is wiser than you are, and that He loves you too well ever to wish you to do anything that is not good for you. If He calls on you to give up anything, no matter how dear, you may be quite sure it is the best thing you can do to give it up. Let it be as dear as a right hand or as a right eye, you are mad if you keep anything of which Jesus has said, 'Part with it'; and the moment Jesus says, 'Part with it', though the thing may be lawful in itself, from that moment to keep it is sin.

Sin, most likely, is very dear to you; not perhaps open and gross sin, but something that displeases God; something that takes His place in your heart; something that you love and serve more than Him. Now one of the greatest of all sins and the root of all others is to 'worship and serve the creature more than the Creator'; for this is to break the first commandment, which says, 'Thou shalt have none other gods before me.' If you have anything in your heart you are not willing to make secondary to God, you are guilty of breaking the first commandment. Christ calls on you to part with that thing, be it what it may, and to put Him in its place; and it is in His wisdom and in His love that He calls. Let it go, and go with this Man, and you will for ever bless God that you let it go. Either it or Christ must go, for it has pleased God that in all things Christ should have the pre-eminence; and it is only mocking Him and deceiving yourself, to say you will take Him, unless you are prepared to put Him before all things. In the instant you accept Christ, your Maker becomes your Husband (Isa. 54:5); and would you expect even an earthly husband to consent to be loved and honoured only in a secondary degree? Can you then think that your Husband, the Lord from heaven – 'the Lord of Hosts is his name, and thy Redeemer the Holy One of Israel, the God of the whole earth shall he be called' – will consent to let you keep your old lords and your old gods, when you say, 'I will go with this Man?'

Count the cost, for the old lords and the old gods must be given up, or Christ must be again refused. I say again – for though I hope to have many readers who have accepted Christ, I expect to have few to whom He has never been offered – you refused Him long ago, for the very reason that makes you unwilling to accept Him now – because if you accept Him you must give up sin. What has sin done for you since first you heard of Christ? Has it repaid you for what you have lost by keeping it? Look at what you are. Look at what you might have been. Let your worldly prosperity be what it may, your best side shows you a forgetter of God, in the full enjoyment of the pleasures of sin; the reverse discovers an unpardoned, unsaved sinner, having no hope, and without God in the world. Your brightest dreams have no wider extent than this life; and let your present happiness be what it may, if your doctor was to put his hand upon your pulse, and tell you that you must die *now,* your happiness would be gone *now and for ever.*

This, at your best estate, is what you are; but what might you not have been? 'Begotten again unto a lively hope by the resurrection of Jesus Christ from the dead, to an inheritance incorruptible, undefiled, and that fadeth not away, reserved in heaven *for you,*' (1 Pet. 1:3, 4). You might have been the child of the Father; the heir of His Glory, the beloved of the Son, and the temple of God. Even these truths, wonderful as they are, do not convey to you all that you might have been. And all this you may be still. Will you be so mad then as to refuse Christ again? You have destroyed yourself, you have doomed yourself, soul and body, to everlasting ruin – but God again offers you pardon and Christ Jesus. Will you again reject His offer? You must give the answer to God, not to me; for it is not I, but He who asks: 'Wilt thou go with this Man?'

Do you ever remember how greatly you are in debt to God? You fancy you can do very well without Christ at present, but what will you do if you have not Christ in the day that God says, 'Pay Me that thou owest?' You may think just now that your sins have not been very great. That, as I have already shown, in the matter of salvation or condemnation makes 'no difference.' I will not again combat that position, but, meeting you on your own ground, I ask you: Did you ever leave a bill unpaid for a year or two, with a creditor from whom you were in the habit of frequently purchasing articles that were individually of small value? I think no man ever did, who was not astonished at the sum total when his bill was sent in to him. Many have learnt to their cost in this world, that debts contracted for small sums, and neglected for long periods, swell to large amounts; sometimes so large that they have found it difficult, yea, impossible to pay them.

Now if this be so with debts on earth, and neglected for a few years, what mind can calculate, even supposing every item to be the smallest, the amount of the debt a sinner contracts in a lifetime with God!

How old are you? From the day you could think and speak until this hour, you have been getting into debt with God. You have never rendered to Him, in any one day of your life, a faithful stewardship of that which He entrusted to you; and you have never lessened, by a single farthing, the amount contracted in the days preceding. Day by day and year by year, you have been steadily increasing your debt, and God Himself has been most honestly and faithfully keeping your account. At this very moment, unless you are Christ's, and He has paid it for you, as these pages are before you, so your debt is before God. Line upon line, page upon page, the register of what each day He entrusted to you, the register of what each day you rendered to Him, is all before Him. No moment of your life has been forgotten – every one is noted there, and described as how spent; and grant the individual items of sin to be as small as you are pleased to call them, your debt to God must now be very large and heavy. It has never troubled you, perhaps, for God has never yet demanded payment; but for all that, the day will come when He will demand it. It may be today, or it may not be for a few years, but come it will; and if, in the day of reckoning, that debt still stands against you, think with what agony you will see the books opened, and the long long pages of that bill unfolded. Your creditor will then demand, – 'Pay me that thou owest.' With what will you meet it? *You will have nothing wherewith to pay.* Those who have accepted Christ, will then be called to sit with Him on His throne; but before you there will be nothing but the debtor's prison, from which you shall in no wise come out till you have paid the uttermost farthing.

Reader, if you are out of Christ, you are greatly in debt to God; and it would be better for you that you had never been born than to appear before God with these debts unpaid. Think, then, I charge you solemnly, before you again reject Jesus. Take Him, just as you are, and He will take you and pay all your debts. O how happy you would feel if you owed God nothing, except to love Him! This will immediately be your position if you will go with this Man.

If you accept Jesus, not only will He pay for you all that great debt you owe to God, but He will give you of His riches; so that henceforth you shall not only have enough for your own need, but 'enough *and to spare.'* This was one of the thoughts that sent the prodigal back to his father: 'How many hired servants in my father's house have bread enough *and to spare?'*

Did you ever reflect on the uselessness as well as the sinfulness of merely living for this world? You may be a hundred years old, but unless Christ has done it in you or by you, you have never done a single act in your whole life that has brought glory to God, or done real and permanent good either to yourself or your fellow-creatures.

This may seem to you a hard saying, but I will prove it from your own case. You are a man who has lived for the world? Yes, you reply, but you are also a living witness that my statement is not true. Whatever may be the case with other people, you have most unquestionably done much real good to yourself. You began life with few advantages, but you denied yourself, watched your opportunities, and made the most of them; and now having lived for some years steadily for the world, you find yourself, though hardly in the prime of life, with rank, fame, fortune, and you know not that you have a wish ungratified. Will I say to you, you ask, that you have not done any real good to yourself?

Oh, brother, if you had lived as steadily for God as you have for the world, you would indeed have had rank and fame and fortune; and durable and substantial would have been the real good you would have done yourself. As it is, the good you have done yourself is a shadow. I will answer your question with another. How long have you to live? You say you do not know. Let me tell you. Your life is co-eternal with God's: *you have to live as long as God lives.*

It is true your life is not to be passed in this world. Your life in this world may be over any moment, and most certainly will be over some moment, 'then whose shall those things be that thou hast provided?' Your life in this world bears a less proportion to the life that is before you, than does the millionth part of a grain of sand to a million worlds crushed into powder; but He who had power to place you here, and who gives no account of His actions to any, has revealed to you that it is His intention to place you in another world – a world as real and actual as the one you now inhabit – with this difference: that whereas this one is temporal and passing away, that to which you are hastening is unchangeable and eternal. It is written, 'This corruptible must put on incorruption, and this mortal must put on immortality,' and you, O reader, whoever you are, have to spend eternity in a world of misery, or a world of glory. Whether it be misery or glory, depends upon what you live for here; and can you be said to have done any real good to yourself, if you have made no provision for eternity, but only gained the things of this world?

You remember the rich man in hell, who being in torments, lifted up his eyes, and cried for water, and the answer he got: 'Son, thou in thy life-time receivedst thy good things.' If you were at this moment in your coffin, would the good you have done to yourself do you more good than 'the good things' he had in this life did the rich man when he was in hell?

A day out of a life-time is a far longer period than a life-time out of eternity; and with greater show of truth might a ruined prodigal maintain through his life of beggary that he had done good to himself in sacrificing his all for a night of mad excitement at the gaming table, as for a man to maintain that he had done good to himself who had pursued and gained nothing but the things of this world. 'What shall it profit a man if he shall gain the whole world and lose his own soul?'

The same argument applies to your fellow-creatures. You may be the greatest philanthropist on earth, with the power of carrying out your philanthropy to your heart's content, but if you have never done anything for the spiritual welfare of your fellow-creatures, you have never done any real good. He who has given away a tract which God has blessed, or spoken a word in season to the saving of a soul, has done more real good on the earth than all the natural philanthropy of all the unrenewed men that have ever lived since the world began.

It is a positive fact that without Christ no man can do real good, either to himself or others. Jesus for ever settled the matter when He said, 'Without me ye can do nothing.' (John 15:5). But take Christ, and not only will He pay all your great debt to God, but will with Himself freely give you all things. What these things are, the Holy Ghost will teach you: for when you take Christ. He will baptize you with the Holy Ghost (John 1:33); and when the Holy Ghost is come, He will take of the things that are Christ's, and show them unto you. (John 16:13–15).

Oh, how very, very rich is the man who has got Jesus! God Himself describes him as 'complete in Him,' and lacking nothing. Accept Him, and you will not only have all sufficiency for yourself, but out of your abundance you shall be able to supply the need of others. You shall be so rich, that you shall have 'enough *and to spare.*'

Accept Jesus, I say again, and with a bounty that has no limit but your own will, you will have the unsearchable riches of Christ to scatter; and with the same truths that made you rich, you may make rich many a poor, needy, helpless, hopeless sinner, now on the road to hell, without even as much knowledge of God's truth as to know that he is going there.

Who is so truly rich upon the earth as he who has the wherewithal to bring glory to God, and to do real good to his fellow-creatures? These riches may all be yours, if you will accept God's offer, and go with this Man.

To do good to others, is an honour that comes from God only. The very desire is Christ-like; and those that are Christ's have both the desire and the power. If you have lived without Christ, you have done nothing either for God or man in the past. If you would now take Christ, what might you not do both for God and man in the future! What a blessing on the earth might you be, who have hitherto been no blessing!

Many a time do I think of what I was, and of what I am – or at least of what I have been since I accepted Jesus. For forty-four years of my life, my object was to pass time pleasantly; so long as the day was spent agreeably I was satisfied. During those years, whatever harm I may have done, I do not believe I ever did any real good to a human being. From 1835 until 1854, with the exception of about three years, the greater part of my time was spent in Scotland, where I rented moors and fisheries. My

102

greatest idea of pleasure was to shoot grouse and catch salmon.

I believe, at the different shooting quarters I rented, I treated the poor with an average liberality, contributing to the different collections what I fancied would be expected, with an odd five shillings when an old woman lost her cow. But what I considered my great act of kindness to the people, and that for which I expected them to be most thankful, was to give them, at the end of the shooting season, a dance and supper. Now let not the philanthropist imagine that I intend to compare his philanthropy with mine. I put his on the very highest scale, mine on the very lowest: only maintaining, that to the recipients of our kindnesses it will be all the same a hundred years hence.

To this party of mine came all the tenants in the neighbourhood, with their wives and their daughters, the gillies, the shopkeepers of the village, my own servants, and all and sundry and every acquaintance that any of these liked to bring. They were very merry. Late in the evening perhaps some were very noisy, and early in the morning I have seen some very tipsy. It would be daylight, perhaps, when a number of both sexes, giving me three cheers, and thanking me for my kindness, would cry, 'God bless you!' and start on their way home.

They thanked me for my kindness; but was it kindness? They cried, 'God bless you!' but could either they or I expect God's blessing on such a meeting? It is true it was intended kindly, and as a return for kindness to those who had taken care of my shootings and preserved my game, and I knew no better way of saying, 'I am obliged to you,' yet again I ask, Was it kindness?

In the end of 1854 it pleased God to bring home with power to my heart, that it would profit me nothing if I gained the whole world and lost my own soul. After much conflict with sin and unbelief, I was enabled to receive the truth: 'The blood of Jesus Christ, God's Son, cleanseth us from all sin.' If from *all,* then, great and many, and to my eyes unpardonable as my sins were, it could cleanse them. So by the grace of God I accepted Jesus, and have now, like the Corinthians, Scripture warrant for saying, I am washed, I am sanctified, I am justified, in the name of the Lord Jesus, and by the Spirit of our God. It is true that I rejoice, and I say it with trembling – for though I have no doubt as to the justification, I am most dissatisfied with the sanctification. Still it is not out of what *I am,* but out of what *He is,* that I am to get my hope, and peace, and joy; and certainly, though I am not what I should be, I am not what I was.

Since I believed in God, it has pleased Him to open to me many doors of usefulness, and instead of a shooter of grouse and a catcher of salmon, I have become a fisher of men. As I used to have at my shooting quarters, so do I still have meetings and gatherings wherever I go; but instead of asking those who come, to dance, I ask them to pray; and instead of feeding them with the meat which perishes, I offer them that bread of which if a man eat he shall never die, and point them to that flesh which 'is meat indeed,' and to that blood which 'is drink indeed.' (See John 6:51–55).

And in the humblest gratitude would I say that it has pleased God greatly to bless these meetings. I am afraid lest I should seem to exalt *myself*; but remember I am not speaking of what I have wrought, but of what *God has wrought,* by a hell-deserving sinner, who has accepted Jesus and tried to scatter the unsearchable riches of His truth. To Him be the whole honour and glory and praise and gratitude for ever. I believe that I, who recorded a few pages back that up to the year 1854 I had never by a single act either brought glory to God or done good to man, may now record that I have done such good to man as shall redound to the glory of God for ever and ever!

Glory be to God that many sinners are now in heaven who first received the Gospel from my lips. Glory be to God that many more are now on their road to heaven, who first received the Gospel from my lips. And glory be to God, I say again, that many of these, my children, have brought others, their children, and consequently my grand-children, to Christ; and these others have brought others, and these others others.

And once more I say, Glory be to God that the sowing and the reaping, the seed-time and the harvest are not yet ended; nor do I believe they will ever end as long as the world shall stand. I have no doubt that the good seed of God's Word which I have been privileged to scatter, and some of the fruits of which I have been privileged to see, will yield seed again, and bear fruit again after its kind. This in turn will seed again, and bear fruit again; and so go on seeding and fruiting, seeding and fruiting, to the glory of God and the salvation of souls, not only when I am in my grave, but until time shall be no more.

Compare the happiness I must feel in being able to write this, with the pleasure the best salmon fishing or grouse shooting could ever give me. Compare the happi-ness and pleasure it gave me when a half-tipsy party shook me by the hand, and cried, after a dance and supper, 'God bless you!' with the pleasure I have felt when, passing through the people after speaking to them about Jesus, some hand, the face of whose owner perhaps I never saw, has slipped quietly into mine, and I have heard the same words whispered, 'God bless you!'

Think not I write these things in the spirit of boasting. To record something of what God can do, and has been

105

pleased to do with the chief of sinners, I think may encourage others, and therefore I record it; but I record at the same time, to my shame, that I believe many of those who call me their spiritual father, are much further on in the Divine life than I am; and I earnestly request every Christian who reads this book to pray that I may keep under my body, and bring it into subjection, lest after I have preached to others I myself should be a castaway. (I Cor. 9:27).

But perhaps you will say that if you accepted Christ you would not have the opportunities that I have had, and could not hope to do the same good. That may or may not be so, as it may please God; but if you will accept Him, you will become a living member of His body, and will most certainly be of use to the body. You may not be a mouth, or any prominent member, but if you become a member at all, you will be a great addition to the body of Christ. 'The body is not one member, but many. If the foot shall say, Because I am not the hand, I am not of the body; is it therefore not of the body? And if the ear shall say, Because I am not the eye, I am not of the body; is it therefore not of the body? If the whole body were an eye, where were the hearing? If the whole were hearing, where were the smelling? But now hath God set the members, every one of them in the body, as it hath pleased him. And if they were all one member, where were the body? But now are they many members, yet but one body. And the eye cannot say unto the hand, I have no need of thee; nor again, the head to the feet, I have no need of you.' (1 Cor. 12:14–21). God forbid that either you or I should ever think of ourselves otherwise than Paul thought of himself, 'less than the least of all saints.' Still, for all that, accept Christ, and be you the weakest thing, or the basest thing on earth, not only will the Head never say to you,

'I have no need of you,' but, while I speak it with reverence, I will add, *you may be quite sure the Head has need of you.*

The believer knows that he is in himself nothing, and owes all that he is to grace; yet this unspeakable glory belongs to the very least of God's people. He is a member of Christ's body, of Christ's flesh, and of Christ's bones, and without him the Body of Christ would not be perfect.

God never chose any man for the service He could get out of him after his conversion. No idea can be more erroneous, and indeed of late years, I know of few that have done more harm than the notion that directly a man thinks himself converted, he must go out and preach. I am far from saying that there have not been, and may not often be cases in which the direct leadings of God bring newly-converted men before the public, but I do say that there are more ways of serving Christ than by public preaching, and I repeat again, that every member of His body is not a mouth. God has laid down this as a general rule, and repeated it twice in four verses: 'Let every man abide in the same calling wherein he was called'; and again, 'Let every man, wherein he is called, therein abide with God.' (1 Cor. 7 : 20–24). I believe that the man who, because he has become a Christian, thinks it necessary to leave a lawful calling and become a preacher makes a great mistake. For all this, however, though a Christian is not necessarily called upon to become a preacher, he is called upon, both by conduct and conversation, to try and win souls to Christ. The commandment is, 'as we have opportunity, let us do good unto all men,' and let no man think that he cannot win souls because he has neither the gift nor the opportunity of addressing large audiences.

Wives and husbands, fathers and children, masters and servants – indeed every one in the position in life in which

107

he is placed – has a special sermon written for him in the Bible, which God expects him to write on his heart, and to preach every day of his life. Let us take, for example, the one written for wives to preach: 'Likewise, ye wives, be in subjection to your own husbands, that if any obey not the word, they also may without the word be won by the conversation of the wives, while they behold your chaste conversation coupled with fear.' (I Peter 3:1, 2). Look at the whole passage for yourself, if you are a woman. God wrote it for your learning. I have quoted enough to show how God expects wives to preach.

The other sermons are somewhat similar, and I leave each Christian to discover them for himself, but first pointing out that this preaching, which God so clearly demands from every man, is far more self-crucifying than public preaching, and in the vast majority of cases will do much more good. Were there a revival in the Church, or in other words, if all who call themselves Christians would daily preach the sermon God has told them to preach, and compel men to take notice of them that they have been with Jesus, I believe it would be a more effectual preaching than much that has been preached lately, and quite as likely, to say the least of it, to lead to an awakening in the world.

Let none think that I mean to discourage public efforts; but while I would not discourage these, I would encourage those who have neither the gift nor opportunity for such efforts, to embrace the Christian's hope and the Christian life, in the full persuasion that in so doing they will not only save themselves, but in God's own way be a glory to God, and a blessing to man.

Do you really mean to say that it is because you think you cannot do much for God or man, that you will not give yourself to Jesus? What do you know about how much God may be pleased to use you? If you take Him, at all events 'all things are yours, and ye are Christ's.' (1 Cor. 3:21–23). All His riches would be yours to scatter, and might you not expect, while endeavouring to preach as God has commanded, that you might, under God's blessing, win one soul before you died?

One soul! Ah, dear reader, how little do you or I know of the value of one soul! God and the devil know the value of souls. Satan thinks it worth while to spare a legion of his angels to keep one soul (Luke 8:30); and our precious Saviour thought it worth His while to die for every soul that is saved.

One soul! Will you not think it worth your while to give yourself to Christ, in the hope that you may afterwards save one soul? If you give yourself to Him, you may from this minute use the Bridegroom's name, and the Bridegroom's riches, as the bride may use her lord's; and if in scattering what you receive, you become the parent of a spiritual child, and save one soul, who can tell the glory you may bring to God, or the good you may do to man?

Abraham never had but one spiritual child. This may seem a strange idea to some, but I believe it teaches us a great lesson, especially not to despise the day of small things. Abraham never had but one spiritual child, Isaac. Isaac never had but one spiritual child, Jacob. Yet if God had not given each of these this one – if Isaac had not been born to Abraham, and Jacob to Isaac, where would have been the twelve tribes of Israel? where would have been the multitude that no man can number, and which is now like the sand which is by the sea shore, innumerable? These all sprang from Abraham's one spiritual child, and God calls them in Scripture the children of Abraham. In the day that God makes up His jewels, how do you know what a father or mother you may be found to have been in Israel, if God makes you the parent of but one spiritual

109

child, if in the days of your flesh you save but one soul?

Wilt thou go with this Man? Again I ask you, Do you really believe there is such a Person as Jesus? If you do not, and abide in your unbelief, then are you without hope; for His own lips of truth have uttered the fearful words, 'He that believeth not shall be damned'; but if you say you believe on Him, then I ask, Will you accept Him? Oh, brother, sister, I beseech you, do! What can another do for you that He cannot? What can you find in another that is not in Him?

Rank! He is King of kings, and Lord of lords. His riches are unsearchable. All power is given into His hands; and let your eyes but once see Him by faith, and you will at once acknowledge that He is 'fairer than the children of men', 'the chiefest among ten thousand, and altogether lovely'. I have already tried to tell you something of His love. I will only now say that it 'passeth knowledge,' and that it changes not. It is as constant as it is incomprehensible; it is from everlasting to everlasting; it is the same yesterday, today, and for ever. 'I will never leave thee nor forsake thee,' is one of the first words He whispers, and He never breaks a promise.

Think of anything you desire, and then ask yourself, If I accept Christ, could not He give it me? You know He could; and if you accept Him, nothing can prevent His giving it to you, *if it is for your good*. From the moment you take Him, He will with Himself, also freely give you all things that are good for you. There is only one reason that will ever make Him keep anything from you, and that reason will be *because He loves you*.

I have done. I have said what the Lord has enabled me, in endeavouring to commend to you my Master's Son. Nothing now remains, but that you say, 'Yes' or 'No,' in answer to God's question, 'Wilt thou go with this Man?'

11: Ungodly Marriages

AS A RULE, I NEVER PREACH OR WRITE AGAINST anything. It is not the best way, I think, to do good. Doubtless it is necessary that the errors and heresies of false religionists should be exposed, and I believe that God has in all ages raised up men specially fitted for the purpose; but for all that, neither argument nor denunciation will ever so effectually dispel error, as will the plain and simple preaching of the truth as it is in Jesus.

There is no rule however without an exception, and I cannot finish this little book without breaking through my own. I must say a few words on a subject that has been on my heart for years, and one I am sure that is too little dwelt on by Christian teachers generally. I must press upon my readers the sin of unequal, or ungodly marriages. The subject on which I have been treating demands it, as well as my own very strong convictions.

Every reader will at once know what I mean by unequal or ungodly marriages. I mean the marriages of those who profess faith in the evangelical truths of the Gospel, with those who make no such profession. 'And Abraham said unto his eldest servant of his house, that ruled over all that he had, Put, I pray thee, thy hand under my thigh, and I will make thee swear by the Lord, the God of heaven, and the God of the earth, that thou shalt not take a wife unto my son of the daughters of Canaanites among whom I dwell.' Well did Abraham know that not only were these marriages sinful, but that they also brought down God's curse upon men; and though they may not have faith enough to believe in the curse, professing Christians in all

111

ages have known that they are sinful. Here, however, the likeness between Abraham and the professor too often ceases. Because he knew it would displease God, Abraham refused to take a wife for his son from the daughters of the people among whom he dwelt; but who can deny that multitudes who call themselves Christians, both marry and give in marriage, without even asking themselves the question, Am I about to unite myself, or give my child, to one who is a child of God?

I said just now that though professing Christians know the sin of these marriages, they have little faith in the curse they bring; but whether they have faith in it or not, in reading my Bible I find no sin there recorded, if we except the sin of our first parents, which has brought greater curse upon the earth, or which is more positively forbidden, both in the Old and New Testament.

What was the crowning sin of the old world? The sin that caused its cup of iniquity to overflow, and for which God withdrew His Holy Spirit from the earth? Let God's own Word answer: 'The sons of God saw the daughters of men that they were fair; and they took them wives of all which they chose. And the Lord said, My Spirit shall not always strive with man, for that he also is flesh: yet his days shall be an hundred and twenty years.' (Gen. 6:2, 3). From the time that He created him until that moment, God had borne with man; never under any provocation had He rendered him evil for evil, but contrariwise, blessing. But now He tells us that He saw 'every imagination of the thoughts of his heart was only evil continually. And it repented the Lord that He had made man on the earth, and it grieved Him at His heart. And the Lord said, I will destroy man whom I have created from the face of the earth.' (Gen. 6:5–7).

Now I do not by any means say that it was for this sin alone that God withdrew from man, and determined to destroy him, but I do say that this is the particular sin mentioned, which provoked God to declare, 'My Spirit shall not always strive with man;' and that *'always,'* as regarded that generation, meant *no more*. God did not indeed immediately bring in the flood. Space was given for repentance. Man's days, said God, shall be an hundred and twenty years. He sent them, moreover, a faithful teacher. For an hundred and twenty years did Noah, a preacher of righteousness, warn sinners of the coming judgment, and direct them to the ark; but the faithful preacher never made a single convert. The Spirit had ceased to strive, and the preaching only hardened. At the end of the hundred and twenty years the flood came, and with the exception of Noah and his family, not one had fled to the ark. Christ Himself tells us that it found the people occupied precisely as they were when God said, 'My Spirit shall not always strive with man.' 'They were eating and drinking, marrying, and giving in marriage, until the day that Noah entered into the ark.' (Matt. 24:38).

'The sons of God saw the daughters of men that they were fair, and they took them wives of all that they chose. And the Lord said, My Spirit shall not always strive with man.' Surely such a Scripture should make those who are tempted to take husbands and wives as they please pause, for who can tell the number that for the same sin have been left by the same Spirit?

When God brought the children of Israel into the land of Canaan, what was His commandment, both by Moses and Joshua, again and again repeated? 'When the Lord thy God shall bring thee into the land, whither thou goest to possess it, and hath cast out many nations from before thee, the Hittites, and the Girgashites, and the Amorites,

113

and the Canaanites, and the Perizzites, and the Hivites, and the Jebusites, seven nations, greater and mightier than thou; and when the Lord thy God shall deliver them before thee . . . thou shalt make no covenant with them . . . neither shalt thou make marriages with them; thy daughter thou shalt not give unto his son, nor his daughter shalt thou take unto thy son.' (Deut. 7 : 1–3). Thus spake Moses.

The teaching of Joshua was precisely similar. On his death-bed he sent 'for all Israel, for their elders, and for their heads, and for their judges, and for their officers,' and repeating the command, told *the consequences of disobedience*. 'If ye do in any wise go back, and cleave unto the remnant of these nations, even these that remain among you, and shall make marriages with them, and go in unto them, and they to you : know for a certainty that the Lord your God will no more drive out any of these nations from before you, but they shall be snares and traps unto you, and scourges in your sides, and thorns in your eyes, until ye perish from off this good land which the Lord your God hath given you.' (Josh. 23 : 12–13).

Now no Scripture is of any private interpretation, nor are these commands, or these judgments, applicable only to God's people of those days. They broke the commandment; they mingled among the heathen, and learned their ways; they took their daughters for their sons, and gave their sons to their daughters; in the end they served their idols, and perished from off the land. And the same thing spiritually, yet literally, is going on amongst ourselves every day. The so-called sons and daughters of God cleave in heart to the children of this world. They make marriages with them. Satan tells them that after marriage they will convert their idol; but God says conversion is His work, and that He will not do it. 'Know for a certainty,' says God (and, oh, it is strong language!), 'Know for a certainty –

know before marriage – that the Lord your God will no more drive out any of these nations from before you.' On the contrary, so far from you converting your idol to your God, he will convert you to his; and that connection, from which, if formed in the Lord, you might have expected, and got blessing, shall be a snare and a trap unto you. He that you put in the place of God shall prove a scourge in your side, and a thorn in your eyes; and unless God, according to the good pleasure of His sovereign will, mightily interpose to save you, the consequence of your disobedience will be that you will return to God no more, but perish for ever. Oh, how many are there who once seemed apparently on the road to heaven, but, having fallen into this sin, are now as apparently on the road to hell!

I believe that one of two judgments has almost invariably fallen on every professor of Christianity who has been guilty of this sin. Either he has lived to regret it through a lifetime of misery, or he has made shipwreck of faith, and gone back to the world. Examples of going back surround us on every side, and though the examples of the more merciful judgment may not be so outwardly apparent (for many an aching heart alone knoweth its own bitterness), yet no one need seek very far to find that also; but where shall we look to find an example of a professing Christian, male or female, who having married one who made no such profession, was afterwards made the instrument of his or her conversion?

Argue with a person who is about to contract such an engagement, and they will tell you what I have before said Satan tells them, that this is just what they are going to do: convert their idol after they are married. But do they? Do facts prove that this often happens? I do not say that it never happens. I think it probable that it does, for God is sovereign, and converts whom and how He pleases; but I

115

do tell you that after much diligent inquiry, I have never been able to find a case of such conversion. In London, in Edinburgh, in Dublin, and in many other large places, I have preached to masses of people in every rank and grade of society; and I have earnestly requested, and that again and again, that any one would write and tell me, if they knew an instance of a professing Christian marrying a man or woman of the world, and being afterwards made the instrument of their conversion. I have at the same time explained my reason for asking this – that I was anxious to ascertain if it ever was the case; and if it was, what proportion these conversions bore to the number of such marriages. I never received but one answer, and that was to tell me that Augustine's mother married her husband before his conversion, and afterwards converted him. Surely if this is the exception, the exception proves the rule.

How can we expect it to be otherwise. Let us look at the conduct of the professor who makes such a marriage. He knows perfectly well, by the Spirit striving within him, that he is about to commit a great and deliberate sin. I say deliberate, because in these cases there are generally at least weeks, if not months for reflection; and if the sin is committed, it is after a long period of grieving, resisting, and at last silencing the Holy Ghost. The Holy Ghost prays, Do not this thing. And what is the answer made to the prayer of the Spirit? A refusal to grant it! If not with his lips at least by his conduct he replies, that in this matter he is determined. He knows it is grieving to God, and contrary to His commandments. He knows it is sin. He knows he cannot expect His blessing on it. Still his mind is made up, and he is determined to do it. He wishes to keep Christ, but he also wishes to keep his idol; and, let the consequences be what they may, he says 'I will not give up my marriage.'

This is virtually his answer to the prayer of the Holy

Spirit: and then he does what? Oh, can anything be conceived more horribly impious, or God-insulting? He turns round, and says to God, O God, I pray Thee, after I am married, convert him or her that I have put in Thy place, and that I will not give up for Thee. And what does God say? Exactly what He said to the Israelites, upwards of three thousand years ago: *'Know for a certainty* that the Lord your God will no more drive out any of these nations from before you; but they shall be snares and traps unto you, and scourges in your sides, and thorns in your eyes, until ye perish from off this good land, which the Lord your God hath given you.'

Consider the fall of Solomon. Solomon was the wisest man that ever lived, and God loved him; but he took to himself wives of the nations concerning which the Lord said unto the children of Israel, 'Ye shall not go in to them, neither shall they come in unto you. *And his wives turned away his heart after other gods.'* (See 1 Kings 11).

What! Solomon, he to whom God had appeared twice, and who had been honoured to build the temple of the Lord – Solomon's heart turned after other gods! Yes; ye have it on the authority of Scripture itself. Solomon disobeyed God in the matter of marriage, and God left him, for a season at least, in the power of his own heart's lusts. What happened? He, the fame of whose wisdom and piety had gone out to the ends of the world, became, in the hands of a parcel of wicked, worldly women, not only one of the chief of sinners, but one of the greatest fools on earth. 'Solomon went after Ashtoreth, the goddess of the Zidonians, and after Milcom, the abomination of the Ammonites!' (1 Kings 11:5).

But it is not on themselves alone that they who sin in the matter of these marriages bring evil, but on the family that God may be pleased to entrust to them. Who can tell

117

the amount of blood-guiltiness with which that professor is chargeable, who for any personal reason what ever, gives his children a parent who is not a child of God. The children of Israel were the family that God had entrusted to Solomon, and who can calculate the evil that Solomon brought on Israel? For his sin God rent the kingdom out of his hand; ten tribes were taken from him, and given to Jeroboam, and Jeroboam introduced sin into Israel, 'to wit, the golden calves that were in Bethel, and were in Dan,' *from which sin they never departed.* Jeroboam, whom Solomon by his sin had made the father of these ten tribes, slept with his fathers, but neither his sin nor its consequences slumbered with him. The sin of Solomon planted Jeroboam in Israel, and Jeroboam planted sin that corrupted every king that succeeded him. *There never was a good king of Israel;* of the very best of them it is recorded 'for he departed not from the sins of Jeroboam, the son of Nebat, which made Israel to sin.' (2 Kings 10:31).

From the time of Jeroboam, though there was occasionally a glimpse of better things in the land of Judah, Judah and Israel gradually corrupted themselves; they mingled more and more among the nations, intermarried with them, learned their ways, and served their idols, until at length God fulfilled His word by the mouth of Joshua, and they perished from off that good land which the Lord their God had given them. It is remarkable, however, that almost every record of increasing idolatry is preceded by a record of an ungodly marriage. Ahab introduced the worship of Baal into Israel, but before he did so he married the daughter of the king of Zidon; and Jehoram introduced the worship of Baal into Judah, but before he did so he married Athaliah.

'Ahab, the son of Omri, did evil in the sight of the LORD above all that were before him. And it came to pass, as if it had been a light thing for him to walk in the sins of Jeroboam the son of Nebat, *that he took to wife Jezebel the daughter of Ethbaal king of the Zidonians,* and went and served Baal, and worshipped him.' (1 Kings 16:30–31). And Jehoram king of Judah, son of the good king Jehoshaphat, married Ahab's child, the daughter of this wicked Jezebel.

The history of Ahab is too well known to need comment. All I will say of him is, that he seems never to have been thoroughly given up to evil until stirred up by Jezebel his wife. But what a lesson for Christian parents is the history of Jehoshaphat! His natural heart believed this marriage to be most desirable; probably he thought by it to make peace between the two kingdoms, and bring back the ten tribes to worship God at Jerusalem; but did it? So far from it, the woman who in his worldly policy he had taken as a wife for his son, afterwards murdered, with the exception of the infant Joash, all the seed royal of the house of Jehoshaphat, and through the instrumentality of her husband introduced the worship of Baal into Judah and Jerusalem.

Now look, I beseech you, at all these consequences flowing out of these ungodly marriages. Had Solomon not contracted them, his wives would not have turned aside his heart, and he would not have built temples in Jerusalem to Ashtoreth and Milcom; and had he not built these temples, the kingdom would not have been rent from Solomon. Jeroboam then would not have reigned in Israel, and there would have been no golden calves.

Had Ahab king of Israel not married Jezebel, there would have been no temple to Baal in Samaria; and had the pious Jehoshaphat interposed to prevent the marriage of Jehoram, he would at the same time have saved the lives of all his family, and kept the worship of Baal out of Judah. These things are all recorded in Scripture for our learning;

and if inspired histories were written now, we may be quite sure that we should find that the same conduct which brought God's curse on His professing people and their descendants in days of old is bringing it still in the present day, on nations, on families, and on individuals.

Where are the ten tribes now? Perished from off the land which the Lord their God had given them. Where is the tribe of Judah? Perished from off the land which the Lord their God had given them. Doubtless they will both be brought back, for the mouth of the Lord hath spoken it, but as yet the ten tribes never have been. The tribe of Judah was. God sent them captive to Babylon for seventy years, and then mercifully brought them back again.

At the end of seventy years a large company of Jews, taking advantage of a proclamation made by Cyrus, returned to Jerusalem, re-builded and dedicated the temple, and kept the passover. Surely these had had a lesson. Having experienced both the justice and mercy of God, they will surely now keep His commandments, and continue according to this their good beginning. So we should have thought: and so they did, until they were tempted. But then they fell – fell again into sin, and that the very sin which from the days of Solomon to the close of the Old Testament history, is shown to have been at the root of all the wickedness of the Jews. Some professing Christian parents, and some professing Christian children, will tell you that these marriages are not sin; but if this is true, then Ezra was not taught of God. But they are sin, and sin by which Satan in this our present day, as he has done in all ages, is destroying multitudes on multitudes of souls.

Read the last two chapters of the Book of Ezra. Space will not allow me to do more than make some extracts. Ezra had just arrived from Babylon, his heart full of love to God and to his brethren. He found the temple repaired, and its

120

worship conducted with apparent piety, as we often see it in the present day, and doubtless his heart rejoiced within him; but how was his joy turned to grief and mourning, when there came to him those who told him, 'The people of Israel, and the priests, and the Levites, have not separated themselves from the people of the lands . . . for they have taken of their daughters for themselves, and for their sons: so that the holy seed have mingled themselves with the people of those lands.' (Ezra 9:1, 2).

Now when Ezra heard this, did he say it was no sin, or did he even in consideration of their having builded and dedicated the temple, and kept the passover, treat it as if it was what the world calls a venial, or light matter? Judge for yourself, by what he said and did. 'When I heard this thing,' says Ezra, 'I rent my garment and my mantle, and plucked off the hair of my head and of my beard, and sat down astonied . . . And at the evening sacrifice I arose up from my heaviness; and having rent my garment and my mantle, I fell upon my knees, and spread out my hands unto the Lord my God, and said, O my God, I am ashamed and blush to lift up my face to thee, my God; for our iniquities are increased over our head, and our trespass is grown up into the heavens. Since the days of our fathers have we been in a great trespass unto this day; and for our iniquities have we, our kings, and our priests, been delivered into the hand of the kings of the lands, to the sword, to captivity, and to a spoil, and to confusion of face . . . And now, for a little space grace hath been showed from the Lord our God, to leave us a remnant to escape . . . and give us a little reviving . . . And now, O our God, what shall we say after this? For we have forsaken thy commandments, which thou hast commanded by thy servants the prophets, saying, The land unto which ye go to possess it, is an unclean land . . . Now therefore give not your daughters unto their sons, neither take their daughters unto your sons . . . And after all that is come upon us for our evil deeds . . . should we again break thy commandments, and join in affinity with the people of these abominations? . . . O Lord God of Israel, thou art righteous . . . behold, we are before Thee in our trespasses: for we cannot stand before thee *because of this.*'

It is easy to see from this prayer how deeply these marriages affected the holy Ezra, and what confession and humiliation he thought such sin demanded. Read the tenth chapter of Ezra, and you will see what action he thought necessary. He never rested till he made Israel put away his sin; and to the shame of the chief transgressors as long as the world shall stand, he has handed down to us their very names.

I believe there are few who have any idea how soul-destroying is this sin; and fewer still who realise how deeply it is implanted in the natural heart of man. Nehemiah carries on the history of the Jews about thirty years farther than Ezra, and Malachi prophesied about thirty years after Nehemiah. Ezra rooted the evil out of Judah in his day, yet thirty years after, Nehemiah found it dominant as ever. Nehemiah rooted it out in his day, yet thirty years after it had again become so prevalent that by the mouth of the prophet Malachi, God sent to tell the Jews he would 'cut off' the man that was guilty of it.

It is impossible to conceive stronger language than that of Nehemiah. 'In those days,' says he, 'saw I Jews that had married wives of Ashdod, of Ammon, and of Moab; and their children spake half in the speech of Ashdod, and could not speak in the Jews' language, but according to the language of each people.' (Can anything more graphically represent the bastard, soul-destroying, God-dishonouring Christianity we too often see in the present day?) 'And I contended with them,' says Nehemiah, 'and cursed them, and smote certain of them, and plucked off their hair, and made them swear by God, saying, Ye shall not give your daughters unto their sons, nor take their daughters unto your sons, or for yourselves. Did not Solomon king of Israel sin by these things? Yet among many nations was there no king like him, who was beloved of his God, and God made him king over all Israel: nevertheless, even him did outlandish women cause to sin. Shall we then hearken unto you, to do all this great evil, to transgress against our God in marrying strange wives?' (Neh. 13 : 23–27).

In Genesis, the beginning of God's Old Testament revelation, we read, 'The sons of God saw the daughters of men that they were fair, and took them wives of whom they would. And the Lord said, My Spirit shall not always strive with man'. In Malachi, the last book of God's Old Testament revelation, we read, 'An abomination is committed in Israel and in Jerusalem; for Judah hath profaned the holiness of the Lord which he loved, and hath married the daughter of a strange god.' And then follow the awful words, 'The Lord will cut off the man that doeth this.' (Mal. 2 : 11, 12).

I make no further comment, but conclude with the words of Paul to the Corinthians: 'Be ye not unequally yoked together with unbelievers: for what fellowship hath righteousness with unrighteousness? and what communion hath light with darkness? And what concord hath Christ with Belial? or what part hath he that believeth with an infidel? And what agreement hath the temple of God with idols? for ye are the temple of the living God; as God hath said, I will dwell in them, and walk in them; and I will be their God, and they shall be my people. Wherefore come out from among them, and be ye separate, saith the Lord, and touch not the unclean thing; and I will receive you, and will be a Father unto you, and ye shall be my sons and daughters, saith the Lord Almighty.' (2 Cor. 6 : 14–18).

Everyone is unclean who is not washed in the blood of Jesus; and if you refuse to obey the commandment, 'Be ye not unequally yoked together with unbelievers,' you have no Scriptural warrant to expect the fulfilment of the promise, 'Ye shall be my sons and daughters, saith the Lord Almighty.'

> 'O daughter, hearken and regard,
> And do thine ear incline;
> Likewise forget thy father's house,
> And people that are thine.
>
> Then of the King desired shall be
> Thy beauty vehemently;
> Because He is thy Lord, do thou
> Him worship reverently."
>
> (Psalm 45 : 10, 11 *Scottish Metrical Version*).

12: Conclusion

I CANNOT CONCLUDE MY BOOK WITHOUT SAYING A word to the poor backslider. You have read all that I have said, and have felt there is nothing in it for you. The way of salvation has been explained to you, and an offer made to you of Jesus, but you long since professed to accept Jesus, and have long known the way of salvation. The vows of the Lord are upon you, but you have not kept them. The lords and the gods you once renounced have regained much of their old dominion, and you have been unfaithful.

If such is anything like a true description of you, your case is indeed pitiable. You have greatly sinned. You have brought disrepute on the cause of God, and dishonoured the name of Christ. The Spirit of God has Himself declared that it would have been better for you not to have known the way of righteousness, than after you have known it to turn from the holy commandment delivered unto you. (2 Peter 2:21).

The Scripture, which calls everything by its true name, calls your sin adultery – spiritual adultery; unfaithfulness – not to man, but to Christ.

You may think little of such a sin. I have heard people who would turn crimson with shame at the very mention of the word 'unfaithful,' if applied to an earthly husband, say of themselves without a blush, that they had been very unfaithful to Christ. But are vows made to God to be thought less of than vows made to man? Your own evil heart of unbelief, not realizing that this union is even more literal, in that it is more lasting than any earthly union, may answer this question as it pleases; but how does God answer it? In His sight it is amongst the most terrible of all sins; nor is there one in the whole Bible, if we except the sin against the Holy Ghost, against which such judgments are recorded.

I do not say God will not forgive it. Blessed, thrice blessed be His Holy name, that even this is amongst the *'all sin,'* from which the blood of Jesus Christ can cleanse; and if we confess our sin, and return to Him, He will in no wise cast us out; but still we may form some idea of its aggravation, when, though His own God-like nature can forgive it, He neither commands nor expects man to forgive it. It is the only sin God does not tell man to pardon. We are taught to pray, 'Forgive us our trespasses as we forgive them that trespass against us'; and He who so taught us tells us, 'If ye forgive not men their trespasses, neither will your Father forgive your trespasses'; but the same Teacher has also said that a man may put away his wife for adultery. Any other trespass against him, God calls on man to forgive, but this He does not ask him to forgive. He knows the greatness both of its insult and its injury, and He does not tax poor human nature so far.

And do you think that God is more jealous for man's honour than His own honour? Do you think that He who has said man may put away his wife for adultery will not put you away, if you commit this sin against Himself? Be not deceived: you may call yourselves Christian, or any other name you please, but he who lives and dies with the guilt of this sin upon him has no inheritance in the kingdom of God or of Christ.

Search yourself, dear brother or sister, lest you be guilty of this sin without suspecting it. So careless are men about the things of God, that many who call themselves by the name of Christ, and would greatly resent your doubting their Christianity, are nevertheless living in it to their souls' destruction. To whom does James give the dreadful title of adulterers and adulteresses? To those who, having professed faith in the Gospel, were for all that living on terms of friendship with the world. Oh, it is strong language, but it is the truth of God: 'Ye adulterers and adulteresses, know ye not that the friendship of the world is enmity with God? Whosoever therefore will be a friend of the world is the enemy of God.' (James 4:4). Thus saith the Lord, and His Word is truth; therefore so sure as this is truth, to call ourselves Christians and to remain in friendship with the world is to be the enemy of God, and an adulterer against Christ. This is not my teaching, but the teaching of the Holy Spirit. I ask you, then, if you are guilty of such sin, will you continue to think lightly of it?

But you do not think lightly of it, you say. On the contrary, you think so much of it that you are sure there is no hope for you. That you think much of it is of the Holy Ghost; that you think there is no hope for you is of the devil. You would not think of your sin at all if the devil could help it. It is a good thought; and if you had committed the unpardonable sin, and were altogether left of God, you would not, and *could not,* have it. It is a sign that He is still waiting to be gracious to you, and will have mercy on you if you will ask Him. *Dare not to despair;* but rather 'account that the longsuffering of our Lord is salvation; even as our beloved brother Paul also, according to the wisdom given unto him, hath written unto you.' (2 Peter 3:15).

Dare not to despair, I say again; that might indeed provoke God to cast you off, for it would be *to make Him a liar, and to doubt the power of the blood of Christ.* But despair not, rather arise, and once more make your peace with God, washing away your sins, and calling on the name of the Lord.

O He is a wonderful God, and has declared wonderful things of Himself! His thoughts are not as our thoughts, neither are His ways as ours. Man cannot pardon this sin, neither does God ask him to; but God Himself can, and will. He 'hateth putting away,' and says to those who have departed from Him – Return! (Mal. 2:16; Jer. 3:12).

Read Hosea 14, and Jeremiah 3. In Hosea, 'O Israel, return unto me,' is God's cry to His children who have fallen by their iniquity; and the Holy Spirit not only commands such to go back to God, but tells them the very words they are to use, and the answer God will make them. In Jeremiah 3, to encourage the hope, and revive the faith of the fallen, what wonderful words have proceeded out of the mouth of God! Read it for yourself, for I will quote but a verse or two. It is specially addressed to backsliders – adulterers and adulteresses against the Lord of Hosts, their Husband: 'Thou hast spoken and done evil things as thou couldest.' Be they what they may, this takes in all your sin, for you cannot have spoken and done worse things than you could. 'Thou hast spoken and done evil things as thou couldest, yet return again unto me, saith the Lord; turn, backsliding children, for I am married unto you.'

Christ was made Man – was made sin – was made a curse – was forsaken of God that He might be able to offer Himself to you. It was love passing knowledge! and in a day that He was precious to you, you accepted Him. Since then, you have broken your marriage vows, and been unfaithful. What must that love be, which still clings to you in spite of all, and now says to you – Return?

For the last time I ask you, *'Wilt thou go with this Man?'*